More of England!.
To Olivia, from Olive (Dorset. U.K).
Christmas 1986

Village Heritage

Village Heritage

by

MISS PINNELL

with the help of

THE CHILDREN OF
SAPPERTON SCHOOL

introduced by

MICHAEL WOOD

ALAN SUTTON
1986

ALAN SUTTON PUBLISHING LIMITED
BRUNSWICK ROAD · GLOUCESTER

First published 1986

British Library Cataloguing in Publication Data

Pinnell, Miss
Village heritage.
1. Sapperton (Gloucestershire)—History
I. Title
942.4'17   DA690.S/

ISBN 0-86299-263-X

Jacket pictures:

front: Sapperton (Pat Pinnell); Sapperton School
photograph, 1908 (Audrey Ricks);
back: presentation of the award in the Bledisloe Cup Competition
with Pat Pinnell, Stuart Bentley and John Green, 1982
(*Stroud News and Journal*); Michael Wood (David Chadwick).

The publishers also wish to acknowledge the marginal illustration
on p.42 as Crown Copyright/RAF photograph;
and the advice of P. Hammond, Education Officer,
Tower of London, *re* details on p.47.

Design and typesetting by
Alan Sutton Publishing Limited.
Colour origination by
Storrington Colour Plates Ltd, Brighton.
Printed in Great Britain.

INTRODUCTION
by Michael Wood

The Sapperton story is part of the common stream of English history. Its roots, like those of so many of our villages and towns, lie far beyond the written records preserved in our libraries and record offices.

When the Romans came after AD 43 there had already been a long history of Bronze and Iron Age settlement in the British uplands. The network of Roman villas we find in the third century all over the Cotswolds arose in a landscape which was already old, and where much clearance had already been done. Whether this part of England contained what we would call villages is not clear. Nor do we know whether Sapperton was by then a recognisable settlement. Its name is unusual; as it stands it is Anglo-Saxon, and therefore comes from a time after the decline of the Roman Empire in Britain (i.e. after AD 410 and after the English newcomers had settled below the Cotswolds and captured the Roman city of Cirencester (AD 577). But the roots of the place may be earlier. The origin of the name seems to be the Anglo-Saxon word for soap, *sape*, a word which is first found in a medical book written in around AD 950, but which may come from the word the Romans used, *sapo*. Combined with the Old English word for 'farmstead', the name then would mean, 'the soapmaker's farm'. Why, you might ask, the need for soapmakers in the benighted 'Dark Ages', a period not normally associated with personal hygiene? Perhaps an answer lies in the village's proximity to Cirencester, which was a great centre of the wool industry in Roman, Saxon and medieval times. Could the soapmaker's estate perhaps go back to the days in the third century AD when Cotswold wool cloaks were exported to the continent and vast quantities of wool from Cotswold sheep had to be washed before being sent to the huge imperial weaving mill at Winchester? At this time a poem in praise of the emperor Constantine even speaks of the 'innumerable sheep flocks of Britain' and their 'heavy fleeces': in the Cotswold sheep, then, we may have a clue to the origins of Sapperton, situated right below the wooded escarpment outside Cirencester – a small part of the biggest industry in early England.

In Gloucestershire, as in many parts of Britain, we now know that some form of organised life carried on from Roman to Saxon times. City life in Cirencester contracted disastrously after the devastating plague of the 540s, but in the countryside, though the villa houses themselves were abandoned, villa estates like those close to Cirencester at Withington and Chedworth may have carried on as working units; towards AD 700 they reappear in the early Anglo-Saxon documents as estates granted to Gloucester churches newly founded by the Anglo-Saxon overlords of the Severn valley, the kings of the 'Hwicce', the old tribal name for the people of the Cotswolds. By then we can detect the pattern of landscape which is still visible today.

From the 680s to William the Conqueror's *Domesday Book* (1086) we have four hundred years of relatively stable rural life, with about as much land under cultivation in 1086 as in the twentieth century. Never heavily industrialised, the Anglo-Saxon landscape of Gloucestershire has survived till today. There are no Anglo-Saxon documents for Sapperton to bridge that long period, but documents for neighbouring parishes give us an impression of how the woods above the village were exploited by landlords like the Bishop of Worcester in the 890s, and how the ordinary peasants of the villages had the right to graze their pigs and cut timber in part of the woodland set aside for them. With this lack of information from Sapperton itself for these years, the children have wisely turned to one of the best accounts of ordinary peoples' lives in the Saxon period, which comes from the Gloucestershire village of Tidenham in about AD 950; out of such struggles England – and Englishness – would emerge.

Such then are some of the possibilities which lie behind the brief first appearance of Sapperton in history, as one of the 13,000 settlements named in William the Conqueror's great survey of England undertaken in 1086, *Domesday Book*. The entry for the village is combined with that for its next door neighbour, Frampton Mansell, and gives a taxable population for both of seventeen villagers,

nine smallholders, and thirteen slaves. If we allow a multiplier of between four and five to account for the wives and children of these people, we get a total population of getting on for two hundred for the two villages. None of these people was free; some clearly represent the last vestiges of the huge slave population of the late Roman period; every person was obliged to do work for part of each week for the Norman lord, Robert of Tosny. Surviving twelfth-century surveys from the next parish to Sapperton, Minchinhampton, show us how strictly the books were kept on such estates during the 'feudal' period, and how strictly labour services and cash payments were enforced on the ordinary workforce; in the same sources we also learn how over half of the old woods above Sapperton were felled in the 1160s, for sale as timber, for charcoal burning, or to open up more land for ploughing. At this time Sapperton may well have reached its peak of population.

From this period onwards we have a continuous record of the village – as we do for so many places throughout England – through medieval manor accounts, poll tax returns, Tudor and Stuart military musters, and on to the nineteenth-century censuses, and the massive documentation of our own age. The task of sifting it all sounds forbidding, but with the limited resources at their disposal, the children of Sapperton have succeeded brilliantly in rooting out the main sources for the story of their village.

It must be emphasised, though, that this is a search which can be done for every place in the country. Obviously each one has a different tale to tell; regional differences are great; often the amount of documentation varies wildly; but all are part of the same tale, whether a Yorkshire pit village, an East Anglian wool town, a drover's stop on the Welsh border, or a lone *tun* on the hills below Dartmoor. Even in highly industrialised areas like the West Midlands the medieval and Saxon past can be uncovered. Any school or group can do such a piece of research, and everybody's angle will be different: that is one fascination of this delightful book.

The book also touches on some of the key problems in teaching history today. For example, do you tell the story from the top looking down (easier because of the bias of the sources) or from the bottom up (harder because the sources are more difficult to locate, and are often untranslated)? These days it is a moot point whether we should look at our history in terms of battles and dates and the 'glories' of Magna Carta, Agincourt and so on, or whether we should be more interested in the (often nameless) workforce who sustained that civilisation, the villagers and smallholders, for instance, who tilled Sapperton in *Domesday Book*; the poor proletariat of seventeenth-century surveys; the 'working class' which emerges in nineteenth-century accounts. Whether our individual 'roots' are Anglo-Saxon, Scandinavian, Celtic, Irish, African, Asian – or whatever combination of these – we *all* share these 'national' roots. Such ideas arise from this study of Sapperton; this is something everyone can do and through it we can gain an awareness of the past without which the present has so much less meaning.

MICHAEL WOOD

As we watch the walkers of our ways,
we realise here a wealth of history dwells
in every field and stone.
As we trace the footsteps of our ancestors
we are grateful that this beautiful village
is <u>our</u> heritage.
We have compiled this guide to share
our joy with the many who have fallen
under the spell of "SAPERE - TUN",
homestead of the soap - makers.

A VILLAGE HISTORY
PRESENTED BY

THE HEADTEACHER & PUPILS OF SAPPERTON SCHOOL

From the beginning of time, walkers have passed this way. Prehistoric men, trading flints, used the 'Cotswold Ridgeway' which ran along Emmerson Lane via Chapman's Cross to Park Corner.

This route was also used by early men as a SALT WAY, bringing salt here from Droitwich.

The Victoria History of Gloucestershire says there was a Roman way through Sapperton before the Romans built Ermin Street to Gloucester.

The Welsh brought calves to sell and fatten by the Calf Way, through Bisley and Chalford.

Our local Cotswold Warden called us the "Spaghetti Junction of the Cotswolds."

To these footpaths you may add the Turnpike road from Stroud to Cirencester, the Canal Tunnel of 1784, and the 1845 railway tunnel still in use.

All these routes brought people to our village in the past, but what reason brings them here today?

PUBLISHERS' NOTE

Village Heritage is presented as it was written. The book is in manuscript, not typeset; the majority of the photographs are Miss Pinnell's own; and the story itself is unbroken by editorial interruptions. From time to time, however, these boxes in the margins will go behind the scenes to show some of the many people, museums and trips which helped to supply the answers and create the setting in this journey into history. The hope is that these will act as an inspiration and a pointer to others and show some of the ways in which so much historical information is in fact readily accessible.

Cotswold Warden, Tom Askwith, gave the school much information on the ancient network of paths and tracks which pass through Sapperton.

Groups of walkers pass our school almost every day.
We decided to question one hundred of them.

We asked them if they would mind telling us why they came.

Their answers fell into two groups:-

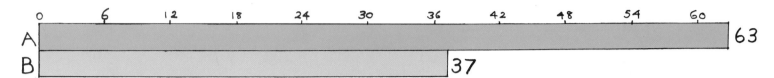

	0	6	12	18	24	30	36	42	48	54	60	

A 63
B 37

Group A, the larger group, said they came because the village and valley were so unchanged by time.

Group B said they came because of events that had happened here in the past, especially the digging of the canal tunnel and the work of the "Sapperton Craftsmen".

In this book we would like to consider these two reasons for visiting us....

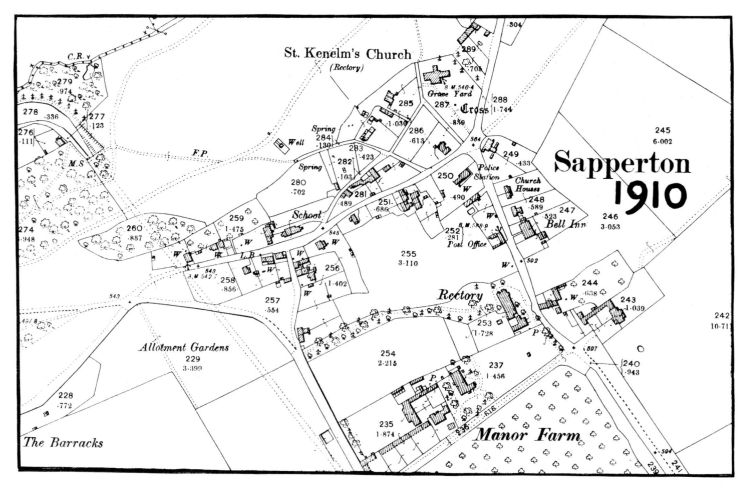

We agree Sapperton only seems to change slowly. If you compare the 1910 map with the 1980 aerial photograph you can see the biggest change in 70 years is the Council Housing Estate in the Glebe.

The Glebe

Russell Adams FRPS and his plane in which he undertakes photographic surveys. Aerial pictures such as this can provide a valuble visual link between a map and the landscape it represents.

Built in 1966, it is probably the largest housing development ever to take place in the village. Great care was taken to make it fit our village style.

<u>But</u>, <u>within</u> our walls our way of life has changed dramatically.

We compared the 1851 census of Sapperton with one we took ourselves in 1982.

The population has halved and many cottages which used to house two or three large families have been knocked into one larger one for a retired couple or people who only come here for the week ends.

One of the original 1851 census forms (from the Gloucester Records Office) together with one of those produced by Sapperton School for their 1982 survey.

8

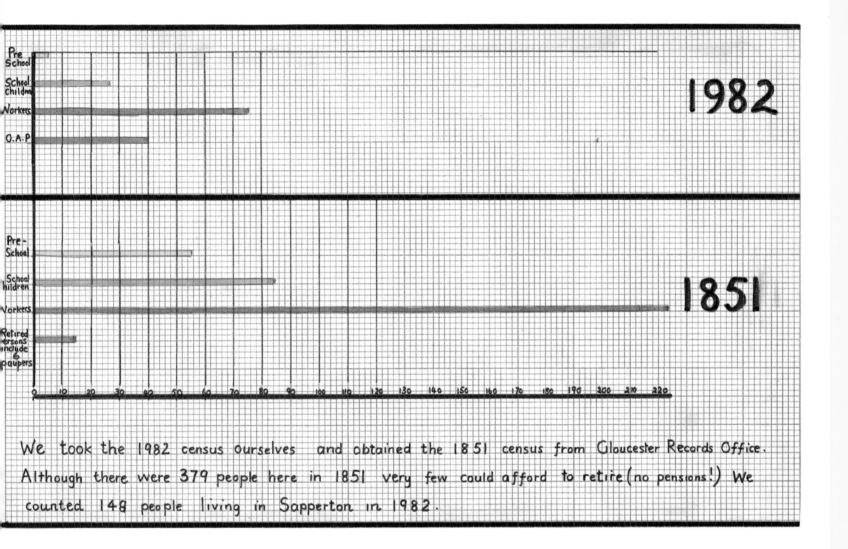

We took the 1982 census ourselves and obtained the 1851 census from Gloucester Records Office. Although there were 379 people here in 1851 very few could afford to retire (no pensions!) We counted 148 people living in Sapperton in 1982.

EMPLOYMENT – Then ...

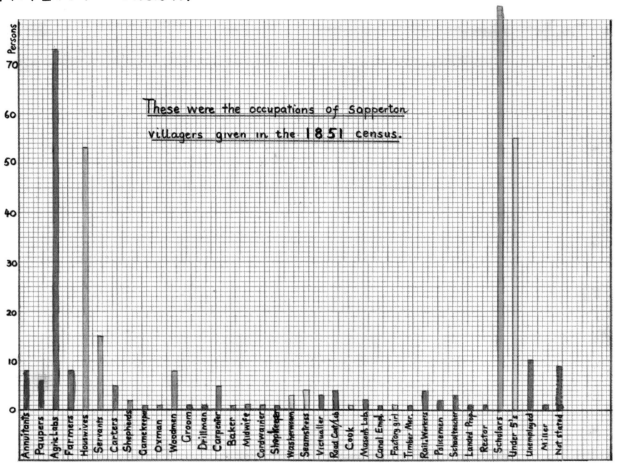

These were the occupations of Sapperton villagers given in the 1851 census.

Persons

Annuitants, Paupers, Agric.Labs, Farmers, Housewives, Servants, Carters, Shepherds, Gamekeeper, Oxman, Woodmen, Groom, Drillman, Carpenter, Baker, Midwife, Cordwainers, Shopkeepers, Washerwoman, Seamstress, Victualler, Road Cont/Lab, Cook, Mason's Lab, Canal Empl, Factory girl, Timber Mer., Rail.Workers, Policemen, Schoolteacher, Landed Prop., Rector, Scholars, Under-5's, Unemployed, Miller, Not stated

Great changes took place in employment between 1851 and 1982. Mechanisation of agriculture and possibly higher wages caused a drop from 73 farm workers in 1851 to only 2 in 1982.

. and NOW...

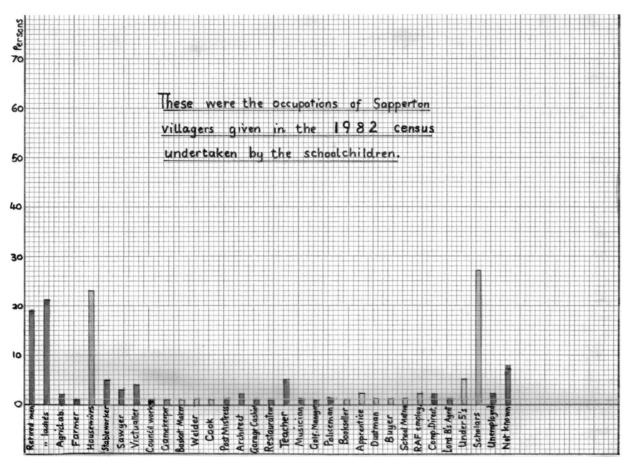

These were the occupations of Sapperton
villagers given in the 1982 census
undertaken by the schoolchildren.

In 1851 there was work for all within the village. In 1982 most wage earners needed to travel
outside the parish. There are few workers about the village by day.

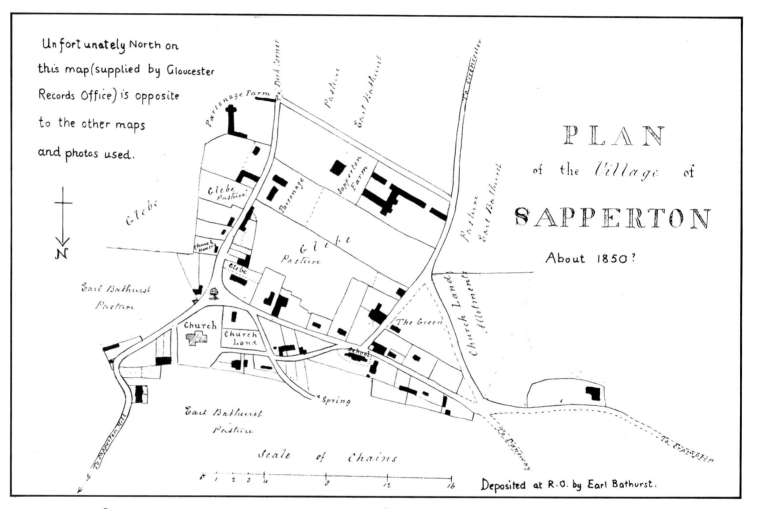

Unfortunately North on this map (supplied by Gloucester Records Office) is opposite to the other maps and photos used.

N

PLAN
of the Village of
SAPPERTON
About 1850?

Parsonage Farm

To Park Corner

Pasture

Ernst Bathurst

To Cirencester

Glebe
Pasture

Glebe

Parsonage

Sapperton Farm

Pasture
Earl Bathurst

Glebe
Pasture

Church Hand?

Glebe

Earl Bathurst
Pasture

Church
Land

Church

Church
Land

The Green

Church Land
(Allotment)

School

Spring

Earl Bathurst
Pasture

To Sapperton Mill

Scale of Chains

5   1   2   3   4   8   12   16

To Daneway

To Frampton

Deposited at R.O. by Earl Bathurst.

On the surface Sapperton has changed very little since 1850. But suppose our population continues to shrink in this drastic way – will we still keep our Post Office? our bus service? our school? What does the future hold?

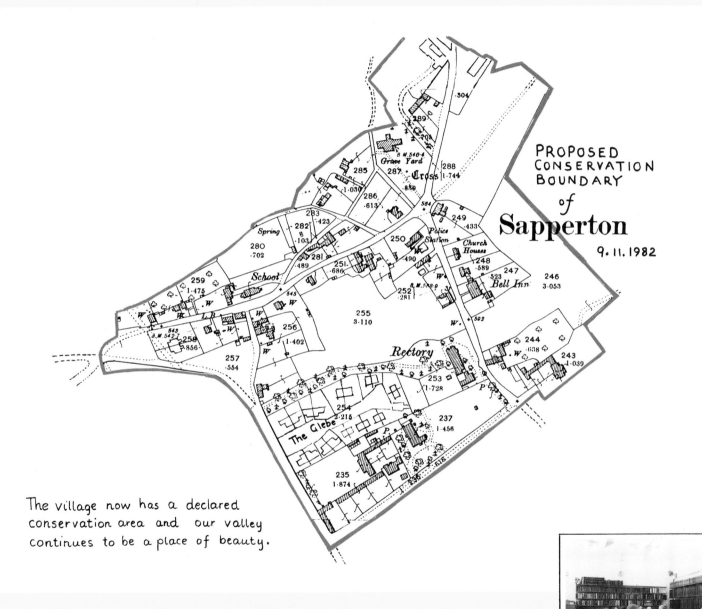

PROPOSED
CONSERVATION
BOUNDARY
of
Sapperton
9. 11. 1982

The village now has a declared
conservation area and our valley
continues to be a place of beauty.

Gloucester Records Office – the source of
many of the documents consulted in this
book. Records Offices throughout the
country make available to the public a
vast resource of regional material – a
goldmine for historical researchers.

So, we think the visitors in Group A who say Sapperton appeals to the
because it is an unchanged village are right, on the whole.
It is <u>within</u> its buildings that the changes have taken place. Life ha
changed for the Sappertonians but there is a strong conservation spir
within the village to preserve its outward Cotswold charm, which
will continue to draw visitors here in future years.

But, for many visitors, including scholars young and old, the mai
purpose of their visit is historic interest (Group B).

Sapperton has welcomed homo sapiens for a very long time. A
fragment of a neolithic Stone Age axe, discovered at Daneway, wa
the earliest artefact found here.

After much research we found evidence of most of the major perio
of history. Some prime sites lie within easy walking distance of th
school and we have noted the positions of the most popular on the
picture on the opposite page.

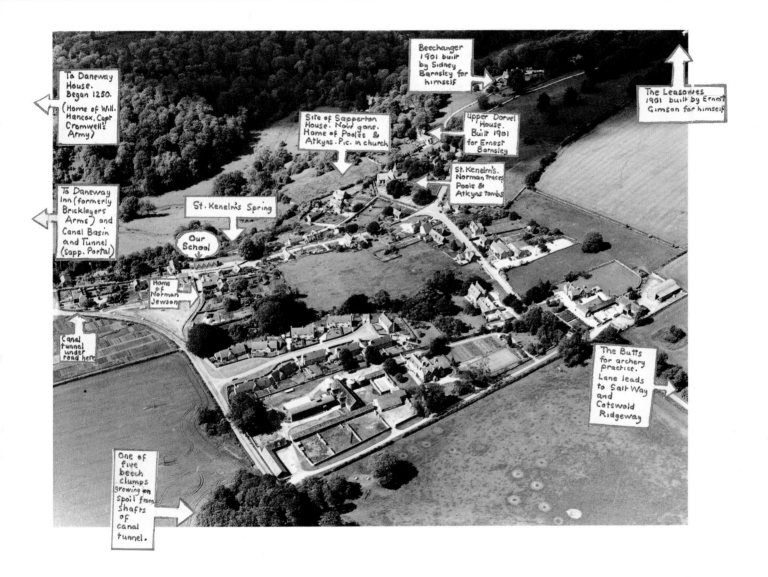

Beechanger 1901 built by Sidney Barnsley for himself

The Leasowes 1901 built by Ernest Gimson for himself

To Daneway House. Began 1250. (Home of Will. Hancox, Capt Cromwell's Army)

Site of Sapperton House. Now gone. Home of Pooles & Atkyns. Pic. in church.

Upper Dorvel House. Built 1901 for Ernest Barnsley

St. Kenelm's. Norman traces Poole & Atkyns tombs

To Daneway Inn (formerly Bricklayers Arms) and Canal Basin and Tunnel (Sapp. Portal)

St. Kenelm's Spring

Our School

Home of Norman Jewson

Canal tunnel under road here

The Butts for archery practice. Lane leads to Salt Way and Cotswold Ridgeway

One of five beech clumps growing on spoil from shafts of canal tunnel.

15

VERY FEW OF OUR VISITORS, HOWEVER, REALIS
JUST HOW RICH IS OUR HISTORIC INHERITANCE
SO....

Come with us as we explore our past.....

The "Victoria History of Gloucestershire" says archaeological evidence suggests that a route through Sapperton and Daneway across the river Frome existed in the late Neolithic period. This is how we imagine the stone-age owners of the axe, found in the garden of Daneway House, may have looked.

The entrance to Hetty Pegler's Tump, near Uley. A visit to this neolithic longbarrow helped to create a context for the somewhat isolated artefacts which have survived, such as the Daneway axe.

Cirencester is approximately six miles away. It is quite possible that a Roman outpost was situated on the rising land opposite Beacon Farm on the main Cirencester/Stroud Road.

It was the law of the Roman Army to take no money into battle. We think a Roman soldier of this camp may have buried his savings here before going on duty and for some reason never returned.

Sapperton children meet the Ermin Street Guard on one of their visits to the Corinium Museum, Cirencester.

The coins lay buried for hundreds
of years.
Their discovery must have caused great
excitement in February 1759, as
you can tell from this account in
"A New History of Gloucestershire",
by Rudder, published in 1775 :-

In the month of February, 1759, there was a large quantity of Roman coins found near a place called Lark's Bush, in the hamlet of Frampton, on a waggon cafually paffing over and breaking the urns that contained them. They had fuffered by ruft as little as could be expected from lying fo long under ground, for they are fuppofed to have been placed there by the Romans. They were foon difperfed into many hands, but no perfon, I believe, collected a more compleat feries of them than Mr. James Dallaway, who has favoured me with the following particulars.

Silver Coins.

Severus Empr. {
SEVERVS PIVS AVG.
Reverfe. A prieft going to offer at a low altar.
Legend. VOTA SVSCEPTA XX. Vows made for the emperor's fafety.
}

Julia, wife to Severus. {
IVLIA PIA FELIX AVG.
Reverfe. MAT. AVGG. M. SEN. M. PATR. [*Mater Auguftorum, mater fenatus, mater patriæ.*]
}

Albinus, commander in Britain under Severus. {
D. CLOD. SEPT. ALBINVS.
Reverfe. Minerva with her helmet, fpear, fhield, and olive branch.
Legend. MINER. PACIFIC.
}

Caracalla Emp. {
ANTONINVS PIVS AVG. GERM.
Reverfe. P. M. TR. P. XVII. COS. IIII. P. P.
}

Plautilla, wife of Caracalla. {
PLAVTILLAE AVGVSTAE.
Reverfe. Two perfons joining hands.
Legend. CONCORDIAE AETERNAE.
}

Geta Cæfar. {
SEPT. GETA CAES. PONT.
Reverfe. The figure of Security refting on one hand, a mound, or ball, in the other.
Legend. SECVRITAS IMPERII.
}

Julia Mæfa. {
IVLIA MAESA AVG.
Reverfe. PVDICITIA.
}

Julia Sœmias, mother of Heliogabalus. {
IVLIA SOEMIAS AVG.
Reverfe. VENVS CAELESTIS.
}

Heliogabalus Emperor. {
IMP. CAES: ANTONINVS AVG.
Reverfe. Mars bearing a trophy on his fhoulder, and a fpear in his hand.
Legend. MARS VICTOR.
}

Julia Aquilia, wife to Heliogabalus. {
IVLIA AQVILIA SEVERA AVGVSTA.
Reverfe. A man and woman joining hands.
Legend. CONCORDIA.
}

Julia Mamæa, mother of Alexander Sev. {
IVLIA MAMAEA AVG.
Reverfe. Juno with her peacock.
Legend. IVNO CONSERVATRIX.
}

Alexander Severus Empr. {
IMP. C. M. AVR. SEV. ALEXANDER. AVG.
Reverfe. Mars.
Legend. P. M. TR. P. COS. P. P.
}

Orbiana, wife of Alexander. {
SALL. BARBIA ORBIANA AVG.
Reverfe. CONCORDIA AVGG.
}

Maximinus Emperor. {
MAXIMINVS PIVS. AVG. GERM.
Reverfe. Peace with her olive branch.
Legend. PAX AVGVSTI.
}

Gordian Empr. {
IMP. CAES. M. ANT. GORDIANVS AVG.
Reverfe. Jupiter with his thunderbolts.
Legend. IOVI CONSERVATORI.
}

Philippus Emp. {
IMP. IVL. PHILIPPVS CAES.
Reverfe. A perfon on horfeback.
Legend. ADVENTVS AVGG.
}

Otacilla, wife of Philippus. {
OTACILLA SEVERA AVG.
Reverfe. CONCORDIA AVGG.
}

Philippus the Son. {
M. IVL. PHILIPPVS CAES.
Reverfe. PRINCIPI IVVEN.
}

Decius Empr. {
IMP. C. M. Q. TRAIANVS DECIVS AVG.
Reverfe. Two female figures reprefenting the countries of the two Pannonias.
Legend. PANNONIAE.
}

Etrufcilla, wife of Decius. {
HER. ETRVSCILLA AVG.
Reverfe. Fruitfulnefs with a cornucopia, and a child by her fide.
Legend. FECVNDITAS AVG.
}

Gallus Empr. {
IMP. CAE. C. VIB. TREB. GALLVS AVG.
Reverfe. Liberty with her cap.
Legend. LIBERTAS AVG.
}

Volufian, fon of Gallus. {
IMP. CAE. C. VIB. VOLVSIANO AVG.
Reverfe. CONCORDIA AVGG.
}

Valerian Empr. {
IMP. VALERIANVS AVG.
Reverfe. Hope with a flower in her right hand.
Legend. SPES PVBLICA.
}

Mariniana, wife of Valerian. {
DIVAE MARINIANAE.
Reverfe. CONSECRATIO.
}

Gallienus Emp. {
GALLIENVS P. F. AVG.
Reverfe. Two captives bound at the foot of a trophy.
Legend. GERMANICVS MAXIMVS.
}

Salonina, wife of Gallienus. {
SALONINA AVG.
Reverfe. VENVS FELIX.
}

Valerianus, fon to Gallienus. {
VALERIANVS CAES.
Reverfe. An infant riding on a goat.
Legend. IOVI CRESCENTI.
}

—— A confecration piece. {
DIVO VALERIANO CAES. In Speed, p. 245.
Reverfe. CONSECRATIO.
}

Valerianus, brother to Gallienus. {
VALERIANVS P. F. AVG.
Reverfe. Vulcan and his temple.
Legend. DEO VOLCANO.
}

Not far diftant from the place where the above coins were depofited, are the remains of a camp, where it is fuppofed thofe foldiers were pofted to whom the money belonged. When this treafure was hid is uncertain, but fome probable conjectures may be formed of the occafion of it.

It was a prudential maxim with the Romans to conceal their money before they were drawn out to battle, or went on diftant expeditions, left any part fhould fall into the hands of the enemy; and becaufe the foldiery had relaxed in this neceffary precaution, it is related by Sparcian, that Pefcennius Niger publifhed an edict, commanding them to carry no gold nor filver coin with them at any fuch time. This money, therefore, muft have been concealed immediately before fome engagement or expedition, from which the owners never returned; or elfe, perhaps, was hid at the time of the final departure of the Romans out of Britain, which happened in the year 476, when, by their troubles at home, they were unable to return any more.

Upon a high fpot of ground, a little foutheaftward of the camp, ftood an antient beacon, wherefore the field is called the *Beacon-field,* and the turnpike-road from Cirencefter to Minchin Hampton and Stroud leads through it, clofe by the beacon-hill.

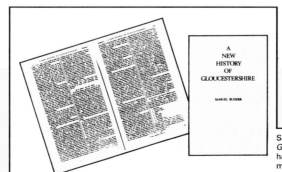

Samuel Rudder's *A New History of Gloucestershire 1775.* Many counties have such histories. Reprint editions make their content more widely available, as in this case.

Sappertonians carrying SOAP to market.

Modern Sappertonians collect the ingredients.

We read that the Romans learned the art of soap-making from the Phœnicians. It seems probable that they shared this knowledge with even the remoter parts of their Empire.

The name SAPPERTON is supposedly derived from SAPERE - TUN, meaning "homestead of the soap-makers."

The children decided it would be fun to experience soap-making for themselves, trying to copy our ancestors.
The curators of our local museums helped us all they could, suggesting mutton fat and a "lye" from burnt bracken as possible original ingredients.

20

Lionel Walrond, curator of Stroud Museum, helping children from Sapperton School.

We burned lots of bracken and saved the ash, which we filtered
to make our 'lye' which we added to mutton fat. Our method may
not have been very scientific but the children will always remember
their SOAP-MAKING.
This activity was most important to us as we believe that it was
at this point in time that Sapperton was born as an

SAPERETUN received its name in Saxon times. "TUN" is an Anglo-Saxon word for homestead or farmstead. Many villages have their name mentioned in a Saxon Charter, but we have not found ours. Country life would be much the same so we were quite pleased to find a Saxon Land Charter for Tidenham, near Chepstow, mentioned in "Anglo-Saxon Charters" by A.J. Robertson. **I**n it, the Manor of Tidenham is granted to the Abbot of Bath by King Edwy in 956 AD. It tells what area it covers (30 hides, each hide being 120 acres of land) and what dues should be paid to the lord of the manor in return for renting land.

Cambridge Studies in English Legal History

ANGLO-SAXON
CHARTERS

EDITED, WITH TRANSLATION
AND NOTES BY
A. J. ROBERTSON

SECOND EDITION

CAMBRIDGE UNIVERSITY PRESS

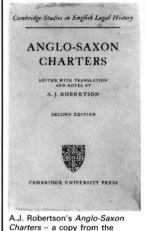

A.J. Robertson's *Anglo-Saxon Charters* – a copy from the Gloucester Reference Library. A mass of Anglo-Saxon documents in translation giving detailed information on dues and land use.

At Tidenham, lying between the Severn and the Wye, fishing at basket weirs was important, so it stated that every alternate fish caught belonged to the lord and every rare fish also.

The community was an agricultural one and the gebur (or villein) had to plough half an acre as week work, reap an acre and a half, mow half an acre, as well as supply 40 rods for weir-building, 15 poles of field fencing and dig one pole of the manor-house hedge. He shall give 6 pence after Easter and half a sester of honey, at Lammas 6 sesters of malt, at Martinmas a ball of good net yarn", and much more, so the lord did well!

ST. KENELM'S, SAPPERTON

24

The Revd Andrew Bowden, rector of Sapperton, who originally suggested the re-enactment of the St Kenelm story. The details came from an account in the church (by James Parker and John Martin).

THE LEGEND of ST. KENELM

Kenelm, patron saint of Sapperton, was a boy king who lived at Winchcombe, around 819 A.D. The legend says he was a victim of his sister's jealousy.

She, Quendryda, covetted the crown and plotted his death...

...at the hands of his cruel guardian, Askobert, in Clent Forest (near Birmingham today). While the Pope, in Rome, was taking Mass, he received a message, by holy dove, to say where Kenelm's body could be found.

The body was lying under a thorn bush in the forest. The Pope notified Kenelm's loyal subjects who went sadly to carry home the body of their much-loved King.
As the procession wended its way to Winchcombe,

springs of water appeared on the way when they were needed.
When Quendryda saw the procession coming, her two eyes fell out upon her prayer book and she died a little while later.

(These scenes are from the story which we enacted at the request of our Rector, Andrew Bowden on Patronal Festival Day to which he invited members of another St. Kenelm's Church, near Clent Forest.)

So many miracles are said to have happened when people called upon his name, that even the springs on the funeral route are said to possess healing qualities.

This spring, being the nearest one to the church, is most likely to be the one known years ago as St. Kenelm's Spring, and as such has provided clear water for many generations of Sappertonians.

It lies just off Church Lane.

1066 – The Normans Come....

Before the Norman Invasion Sapperton was ruled by Ulfe, third son of King Harold. The coming of the Normans was to change all that.

The Bayeux Tapestry, providing perhaps the best-known picture of the invading Normans.

As the Normans rode over the land, King William rewarded his knights with gifts of the conquered villages. Sapperton became such a reward.

So Sapperton ceased to be owned by Ulfe and came into the possession of Robert de Todini; one of William's men from Tosny, a village on the Seine. He also received the Vale of Belvoir and built Belvoir Castle.

XLVI. TERRA ROBERTI DE TODENI *In Salemanesberie* HD.
Rotbert de Todeni ten *Risendone*. Vlf tenuit
Ibi . xiii . hidæ geld . In dñio funt . iii . car . 7 xxiii . uilti
7 vi . bord cū . x . car . Ibi . viii . inī feruos 7 ancillas.
7 molin de . x . fol . 7 uñ burgfis in Glouuecest de . iii . den.
Valuit . xii . lib . M. x . lib. *In Griboldestov* HD.
Ifd Robt ten *Horedone* . Ibi . x . hidæ geld . Vlf tenuit.
In dñio funt . iii . car . 7 xi . uilti 7 viii . bord . cū . viii . car.
Ibi . vii . ferui . 7 molin de . vi . folid . 7 xx . ac pti . Silua . ii . leuū
lg . 7 una lar . Valuit . xii . lib . modo . vii . lib . *In Biselege* HD.
Ifd Robt ten *Sapletorne* . 7 *Frantone* . In uno . v . hide.
7 in alio . v . hidæ . Vlf tenuit . In dñio funt . vii . car . 7 xvii.
uilti 7 ix . bord . cū . x . car . Ibi . xiii . ferui . 7 ii . molini
de . vi . folid . Silua dimid leuua lg . 7 ii . qz lar.
H . ii . M T.R.E . ualb . xiiii . lib . fimul . Modo . xvi . lib.
XLVII. TERRA ROBERTI DISPENSAT *In Grftestane* HD.
Rotbert difpenfator ten *Wicvene* . Ibi . x . hidæ geld.

It is fascinating to read the name of Sapperton (SAPLETORNE) on this page from the Domesday Book.
Written in Latin in 1086, this was a survey ordered by William of the land he had conquered and was compiled because he wished to know the value of what he now ruled.

LAND OF ROBERT OF TOSNY

In SALMONSBURY Hundred

Robert of Tosny holds (Great) RISSINGTON. Ulf held it. 13 hides which pay tax. In lordship 3 ploughs;

23 villagers and 6 smallholders with 10 ploughs.
8 slaves, male and female; a mill at 10s.
1 burgess in Gloucester at 3d.

The value was £12; now £10.

In GRUMBALDS ASH Hundred

Robert also holds HORTON. 10 hides which pay tax. Ulf held it.
In lordship 3 ploughs;

11 villagers and 8 smallholders with 8 ploughs.
7 slaves; a mill at 6s; meadow, 20 acres; woodland 2 leagues long and 1 wide.

The value was £12; now £7.

In BISLEY Hundred

Robert also holds SAPPERTON and FRAMPTON (Mansell). 5 hides in one, and 5 hides in the other. Ulf held them. In lordship 7 ploughs;

17 villagers and 9 smallholders with 10 ploughs.
13 slaves; 2 mills at 6s; woodland ½ league long and 2 furlongs wide.

Value of these two manors together before 1066 £14; now £16.

LAND OF ROBERT THE BURSAR

In GRESTON Hundred

Robert the Bursar holds CHILDSWICKHAM. 10 hides which pay tax.

---

ve is a 1982 translation of our Domesday mention, by John S.

re, but as early as 1712 Sir Robert Atkyns, our

Sapperton historian presented a fuller version

is book " The Ancient and Present State

Gloucestershire," adding his own details

the translation.

SAPERTON.

THIS PARISH lies in the Hundred of *Bisley*, 4 Miles diftant Weft from *Cirencefter*, 3 Miles Eaft from *Bisley*, and 11 Miles South from *Glofter*. ————

" *Ulfe* held *Sapletone* and *Frantone*,
" in *Bislege* Hundred, in the Reign
" of King *Edward* the Confeffor. He
" was third Son of King *Harold*, and
" therefore in the Reign of King *Willi-*
" *am* the Conqueror, he was deprived
" of thefe Mannors, and confined, *&c.*
" and they were given to *Robert de*
" *Todeni*. Each of thefe Mannors was
" taxed at 5 Hides; there were 17
" Plow-Tillages, whereof 7 were in
" Demean: there were 2 Water-Mills,
" and a Wood half a Mile in length,
" and 2 Furlongs in breadth. The two
" Mannors paid a yearly Rent of 14 *l.*
" in King *Edward's* Reign; they paid
" 16 *l.* yearly in King *William's* Reign.
Domefday Book.

Robert de Todeni gave a Plow-Tillage in *Saperton* to the Priory which he had founded at *Belvoir* in *Lincolnfhire*, to pray for the Soul of *Adela* his Wife. He dyed feized of *Rifendon*, *Horedone*, *Saperton* and *Frampton*, in *Glofterfhire*, 1088, and was fucceeded by *William* his Son and Heir, who chang'd his Name, and was ftiled *William de Albini*, with the Addition of *Breto*, to diftinguifh him from *William de Albini* who was chief Butler of the Realm.

John S. Moore's parallel text of the Gloucestershire Domesday entries, one of Phillimore's series of volumes providing the public with a modern translation of King William's survey.

It is only here, in the North Transept of the Church, that traces of our Norman ancestors still linger. Even so, only the jambs of the small doorway and the base of the tower are thought to have survived from the Norman church, because there was much re-building here in the 14th century as the central tower, spire and roofs of the nave and chancel date from this time. (The rest was remodelled in the reign of Queen Anne.)

The Place-Names of Gloucestershire by A.H. Smith. This is Volume XXXVIII of the English Place-Name Society series published by Cambridge University Press and covering the origins of place names throughout the country.

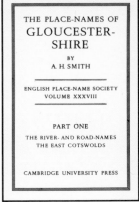

THE PLACE-NAMES OF
GLOUCESTER-
SHIRE
BY
A. H. SMITH

ENGLISH PLACE-NAME SOCIETY
VOLUME XXXVIII

PART ONE
THE RIVER- AND ROAD-NAMES
THE EAST COTSWOLDS

CAMBRIDGE UNIVERSITY PRESS

To the north-west of Sapperton village the land slopes quite sharply down to the Frome. Several routes seem to find it natural to cross the water here. Its very name - DANEWAY - seems to echo of pre-Norman raiding parties, though its other early spelling of "Denneway" belies this and "The Place-Names of Gloucestershire", by A.H. Smith, says that it means "Road through the Valley", referring to a lane leading up a small valley on the north side of the Frome. In "Highways and Byways in Oxford and the Cotswolds" (1905), Herbert A. Evans writes fascinatingly but erroneously of Daneway :-

"As to the name, it may go back to the year 894, when the Danes made a dash up the Thames valley from their stations in East Anglia with the intention of seizing some haven in the Bristol Channel, and there meeting with their ships which were detained by Alfred on the coast of South Devon. In their march from the Thames to the Severn, it is permissible to guess that, like the canal and railway in after generations, they made their way down this valley and left their name behind them. Their fleet, however, they did not meet and after waiting in vain for some time, they were defeated at Buttington, a spot on that narrow neck of land between Wye and Severn."

It is on this spot- DANEWAY- that about 1250 A.D. a start was made on a building which was to become a fascinating item of Sapperton's heritage, Daneway House.

Daneway House, built between 1250 and 1300 A.D., has been continuously inhabited. From 1397 to 1860 the Hancox family lived there.

Originally built as a one-storey hall, it is a good illustration of the development of the English house. It must have been rather uncomfortable, having no chimneys or glass in the pierced stone windows.

The hearth was in the middle of the floor, and the smoke filled the roof-space above the tie-beams, blackening the timbers with soot before it filtered out from a few triangular holes in the roof. These vents remain, now glazed over, in the raftered attic of Daneway House.

35

Lady Denny opened her house to the children and supplied much of the historical and architectural detail.

"Visitors to Daneway"?

About fifty years after it
erection, the upper half was
divided off from the downst
at one end only, not near the
fire.
To get to this upper room or
SOLAR, stone steps were buil
up the outside.
The narrow windows, which
were removed during this
operation, were not wasted.
You can see them today, cut
from one piece of stone,
being used in an out-
building.

The roof of the 13th-century building nestles among the oratory (1339), the gabled High Building (1620) and the projecting porch of 1717.

The pair of pierced lancet windows were probably from here.

Inside that roof-space the rough beams are soot-blackened.

The 'High Building' (early 17th century) has a single room on each ← of its five floors. These rooms are joined by a spiral staircase. Some of the rooms have decorated plaster ceilings and the ...

...Hancox family show their pride in their breed of shire horses by including these in a frieze near one of the doors. We will read more of the Hancox family later.

Sophy Wanny.

SAPPERTON in the 14th & 15th Centuries.

Now we come to a frustrating period in our village story, namely the 14th and 15th centuries. We are told that much of the Church is 14th century: the central tower, spire and roofs of the nave and chancel (and the chimney of the heating chamber which was moved from Henwood Mill), so we do have a few bare bones to go on, but we like our history figures to have a little more flesh on them.

Who was prepared to spend so much money on our Church? Since the Norman Conquest the Manor of Sapperton had passed from father to son (except for a slight hiccup between 1166-1187) until the death of Alard le Fleming in 1263 when he shared it between his two married daughters Joan (Hussey) and Florence (de Lisle).

Thus we get two smaller estates - the Hussey moiety, known as Daneway, and the de Lisle moiety - running side by side till 1463 when the de Lisles sold out to Sir William Nottingham, who in 1480 was able to buy the Hussey portion and unite Sapperton once more.

So, during these 200 years, which of the de Lisles was responsible for the Church re-building? Was it William (d.1345) or Walter (d. 1352) or some other who gave us this lovely ogee-arched tomb recess under the North Tower arch?

In 1348 one man out of every three in England died of the Plague, called the Black Death.

Did the disease reach Sapperton?

At this time many landowners turned their farms over to sheep to save labour and to meet the demand for English wool. Did this happen here?

In the field south-east of the Church (by the present 'phone-box) in the course of a B.B.C. TV programme on our valley, the commentator said he thought it possible that here lay the medieval heart of the village, though to our untrained eyes no traces remain.

If this was so, when did the houses fall into dis-use? Did disaster strike, or was the move westwards a gradual one? This churchyard cross is early 15th century — if these stones could only speak!

We had a stroke of luck!
The Curator of Stroud Museum,
Lionel Walrond, recalled that
T.V. programme ten years ago.
He told us the commentator
was an eminent archaeologist,
Dr. Peter Fowler, Secretary of the
Royal Commission on Historical
Monuments.

When we wrote to Dr. Fowler
we received this kind letter by
return post. Immediately we
hurried to the field by the
Church and were able to pick
out the continuation of the
village street. This winter
we will look for the footings
of the medieval houses.

Royal Commission on Historical Monuments (England)
Fortress House 23 Savile Row London W1X 1AB

Telephone 01-734 6010

Miss P M Pinnell
Gloucestershire Education Committee
The C. of E. School
Sapperton
Nr Cirencester
GLOS

Your reference

Our reference
HO/9/15
Date
11 September 1985

Dear Miss Pinnell,

Thank you for your letter of August 31st about Sapperton and my throw-away
remarks about the field immediately east of the Church. Never did I think then,
on what was a glorious summer's morning that, ten years later, I would be
called to account!

Anyway, I remember the television programme and the field very clearly indeed
and can therefore confirm that the field you mark as 'possible site of medieval
village?' is indeed the place where I saw what I took to be the slight earthworks
of the continuation of the village street in a north-easterly direction with low
walls on either side of it representing the footings of medieval buildings,
almost certainly houses. I remember that with one particularly clear building
site I was able to demonstrate the position of the door, represented by a slight
gap in the line of the wall facing on to the shallow hollow-way. I don't recall
actually saying that these remains were 'probably the medieval part of the
village'; probably the village was much larger than now in medieval times and
these earthworks represent the eastern end of the village, now abandoned.
Alternatively, since we know that settlements tend to slide and slip around the
landscape, it could have been the main part of the village at one time, the
centre of it having subsequently moved to the west. I am guessing here because
I left the Bristol area soon after that programme and have not been able to
follow up at all my interest in your area stimulated by that one visit. I am
therefore not in a position to pass any judgement as to whether or not Henry
Hussey could have lived in this field; in any case, attempts at correlating a
specific documentary reference such as yours with archaeological remains are
fraught with difficulty and dangers. But I am certain, unless my memory is
completely at fault, that, as is the case in many other villages close to the
Church, settlement remains exist in the southern half of that field and that
they give all the appearance of being medieval. Have a look at it in the coming
winter when the grass is right down and I think you will see very low (c. 25 cm?)
banks and depressions forming a rectilinear pattern either side of the shallow
ditch-like feature running north-eastwards from the gate opposite the gate into
the Churchyard.

Here we are, working on the medieval road. Dr. Fowler's colleague, Miss K. Hallworth, suggested that we wrote to the Ministry of Defence, St. George's Road, Harrogate for, according to her records, a sortie No: 3G/TUD/UK 102 had been flown over this field on March 30 th 1946.

She thought, looking at the prints she held, which were on a rather small scale 1/10000, some faint evidence could be seen.

In due course the Ministry of Defence supplied the aerial photograph reproduced here. Shallow ditch-like features could indeed just be detected on the enlarged print. The Royal Air Force Film Library holds extensive world-wide coverage of black and white aerial photography and offers a search facility for particular areas of interest.

This is a list of people living in Sapperton and Frampton (Mauncel) in the year 1327 who were wealthy (?) enough to pay tax. The tax was one fifteenth of their total wealth. We found the names on the "Gloucestershire Subsidy Roll 1327" (In the reign of Edward III) at the Record Office, Gloucester. Over the page are the lists for Coates & Rodmarton for comparison.

EDW. iii., 1327.   29

SAPERTON.

Do. Henr. le Hcose xi s
' Willo. de Insula viii s i d ob
' Rico. Lege xii d
' Walto. atte Forde ii s viii d ob
' Anselim. Pegoys xxi d ob
' Nicho. Pegoys xvi d
' Matill. la Smyth xxii d
' Johe. Gille ix d
' Willo. de Haille iii s ix d ob
' Alic. la Reue xv d
' Rado. Cherug xx d
' Willo. Toce iiii s iii d ob

prob. Sma. xxxix s. vii d. q.

FROMPTON.

' Willo. Maunsel iiii s
' ' Margar Maunsel xviii d
' ' Willo Port ii s q
' ' Henr. Bletz xv d
' ' Henr. Michel xx d
' ' Johe. l'ethet xii d
' ' Alic. atte Steerte xviii d
' ' Pho. Stouke xviii d
' ' Rico de Chirinton xxii d

prob. Sma xvi s. iii d. q.

Henry Husee.

Inquisition taken before *Simon Basset*, escheator [*etc.*], at Saperton, on Thursday, the Feast of Holy Innocents, 20 Edward III [1346], by the oath of *John de Monemowe, John de la Felde* of Pagenhulle, *Richard le Clerkessone, John in la Felde* of Lupezate, *Robert de Eggesworthe, William le Vyleyn, Robert Stonhenge, Robert le Skay, Thomas Roberd, Robert Crouste, Thomas Mody,* and *Henry Zaneworthe,* who say that

It will be no damage to the King or others to allow *Henry Husee* to grant the moieties of the manors of Broderisindone and Saperton to *Thomas de Schirbourne,* parson of the church of Saperton, and *Robert de Teyntone,* parson of the church of Broderisindone, for the purpose of re-enfeoffing the said *Henry* for his life, with remainders in tail successively to his sons *Henry* and *Richard,* his heirs by his wife *Katherine,* his daughter *Elizabeth,* and finally to *John de Huntyngfeld.*

The said moieties are held of the King in chief by knight service; the moiety of Broderisindone is worth 66*s.* 8*d.* yearly, that of Sapertone 43*s.* 3*d.* The said *Henry* holds nothing beyond the said moieties in "my bailiwick."

Chan. Inq. p.m., Ser. I, 20 Edward III, 2nd Nos., No. 2.

New reference, Chan. Inq. a.q.d., File 280, No. 2.

The Curator at Stroud Museum discovered this investigation from the "Inquisitiones Post Mortem for Glos". (Reprinted by the Bristol & Glos. Archaeological Soc. 1903). It states that: how Henry Hussey the richest man on the Sapperton List (estate value 43s. 3d.) wished to leave his estate, would cause "no damage to the King".

43

In the year 1327 these people were alive and paying taxes in Coates, Tarlton, Rodmarton, Sapperton and Frampton Mansell.

In that year Edward II was murdered in Berkeley Castle and buried in Gloucester Abbey (Cathedral). When Edward III became King he ordered these Subsidy Rolls be compiled, rather like William I had ordered the Domesday Book, to know the value of his kingdom.

A costume like this could be seen walking to Gloucester Abbey.

VILLATA DE COTES, ET TORLTONE TRUSSEBURI, ET HUNLACIDE MEMBR.

' Walto. Wilkynes xix d o q
' Matill. de Lullebroke viii s i d o
' Johe. Cokerel iiii s iiii d
' Johe. de Wysham xvii d
' Pho. de Cotes xviii d
' Walto. de Cirencestre ii s i d
' Thom. atte Yate iiii s viii d
' Willo. de Trosburi xii d
' Johe. Reed xiii d
' Alic. Doun ii s
' Alic. Walshe xiiij d
' Walto. Bonvyle xii d
' Matill. Elemore iii s ix d
' Johe. Alderman xii d
' Johe. Kaym xiiii d
' Cristina de Hunlacyde vii s
' Johe. de Munden vi s
' Johe. de Colkerton iii s i d
' Rico. Lacy ii s i d
' Johe. Bovetoun xx d
' Rico. Kaym xviii d
' Alic. Dykes vii s vi d
' Nicho. de Haylegh xii d
' Rico. le Whight xvi d
' Walto. Averay xviii d
' Simon. Spekke iiii s iiii d
' Juliana la Wight xxiii d

prob. Sma. lxxiiii s. x d. q.

27 persons paid ↑
74s 10d, averaging
2s 9¼d each.

RODMERTON.

' Thom. Bovetoune xxii d
' Rico. Inthelane x d
' Reginaldo de Lanyfole xi d
' Alic. la Hopere xx d
' Thom. le Hopere xii d
' Robo. Bovetoun xv d
' Willmo. Burdon x d
' Robo. le Reve xxi d
' Walto. Curteis ix d
' Robo. le Wetherherde vi d
' Johne. Burdon xvi d
' Willmo. le Welsshe vi d
' Thom. le Prest xii d
' Nicho. Inthelane xiii d
' Stepho. de Clenchcham ii s

prob. Sma. xvii s. iii d. o.

15 persons paid ↑
17s 3d, averaging
1s 1¾d each.

SAPERTON

Henr. le Heose xi s
Willo. de Insula viii s i d ob
Rico. Lege xii d
Walto. atte Forde ii s viii d ob
Anselim. Pegoys xx i d ob
Nicho. Pegoys xvi d
Matill. le Smyth xxii d
Johe. Gill ix d
Willo. de Haille iii s ix d ob
Alic. la Reue xv d
Rado. Cherug xx d
Willo. Toce iiii s iii d ob

prob. Sma. xxxix s viii d q.

12 persons paid ↑
39s 6½d, averaging
3s 3½d each.

FROMPTON

Willo. Mauncel iiii s
Margar. Mauncel xviii d
Willo. Port ii s q
Henr. Bletz xv d
Henr. Michel xx d
Johe. Pethet xii d
Alic. atte Steerte xviii d
Pho. Stouke xviii d
Rico. de Chirinton xxii d

prob. Sma. xvi s iii d q.

9 persons paid ↑
16s 3d, averaging
1s 9½d each.

By these figures, Sapperton would appear to be comparatively wealthy in 1327.

While Daneway House had been growing to its present state, life had continued apace in Sapperton itself. Heirs of its Norman overlords had come and gone; the feudal system shaped the whole community and a line of rectors from 1234 sustained the life of the Church.

In 1483, Sir William Nottingham, Lord of the Manor of Sapperton, died and his widow married Richard Pole, thus introducing a name that was to be of great importance to Sappertonians for the next two hundred years:-

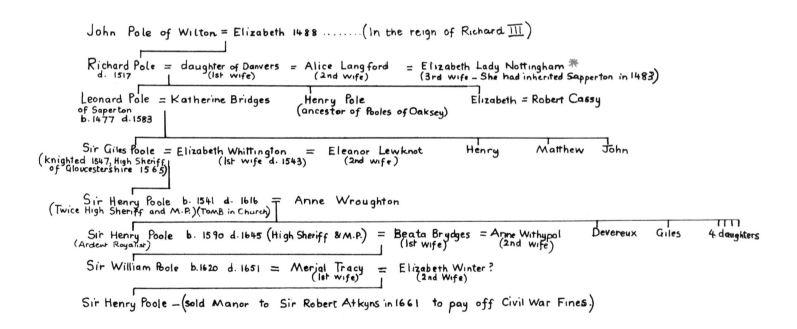

John Pole of Wilton = Elizabeth 1488 ....(In the reign of Richard III)

Richard Pole = daughter of Danvers = Alice Langford = Elizabeth Lady Nottingham
d. 1517   (1st wife)   (2nd wife)   (3rd wife – She had inherited Sapperton in 1483)

Leonard Pole = Katherine Bridges   Henry Pole   Elizabeth = Robert Cassy
of Saperton   (ancestor of Pooles of Oaksey)
b.1477 d.1583

Sir Giles Poole = Elizabeth Whittington = Eleanor Lewknot   Henry   Matthew   John
(knighted 1547, High Sheriff,   (1st wife d. 1543)   (2nd wife)
of Gloucestershire 1565)

Sir Henry Poole b. 1541 d. 1616 = Anne Wroughton
(Twice High Sheriff and M.P.)(Tomb in Church)

Sir Henry Poole b. 1590 d. 1645 (High Sheriff & M.P.) = Beata Brydges = Anne Withypol   Devereux   Giles   4 daughters
(Ardent Royalist)   (1st wife)   (2nd wife)

Sir William Poole b.1620 d. 1651 = Merjal Tracy = Elizabeth Winter ?
                                   (1st wife)   (2nd Wife)

Sir Henry Poole — (sold Manor to Sir Robert Atkyns in 1661 to pay off Civil War Fines.)

In the unsettled reign of James I, shortly after the thwarted Gunpowder Plot of 1605, the King ordered all towns and villages to undertake a census of males.

He wished to know who he would be able to call upon should he need to raise an army in a hurry.

<u>This census would show the height, age and occupation of every able-bodied man in England</u>. It would also show what arms and armoury the nobility could provide if required.

In his book "Men and Armour for Gloucestershire in 1608," John Smith gives the following details :-

Men and Armour for Gloucestershire in 1608

THE names and Surnames of all the able and sufficient men in body fitt for his Ma'ties service in the warrs within the City of Gloucester and the Inshire of the same, wherein are contayned the City of Glouc' and the Hundreds of Dudstone and Barton Regis, with their ages, parsonable Statures and Armours viewed by the Right honorable Henry Lord Barkley Lord Lieutenant of the said City and the County thereof by direction from his Ma'tie in the month of September, 1608. Annoq' Sexto Regni Regis Jacobi Anglie &c. Wherin Observe viz. That

The figure (1.) sheweth the age of that man to bee about Twenty.

The figure (2.) sheweth the age of that man to bee about fforty.

The figure (3.) sheweth the age of that man to bee betwene fyfty and threescore.

The L're (p.) sheweth the man to bee of the tallest stature fitt to make a pykeman.

The L're (m.) sheweth the man to bee of a middle stature fitt to make a musketyer.

The L'res (ca.) sheweth the man to bee of a lower stature fitt to serve with a Calyver.

The L'res (py.) sheweth the man to bee of the meanest stature either fit for a pyoner, or of little other use.

The L'res (tr.) sheweth that at the takinge of this viewe, bee was then a trayned soldyer.

The L'res (sub.) sheweth that the said man was then a subsidy man.

Children from Sapperton visit the Folk Museum in Gloucester to look at armour from the time of the Civil War. John Smith's book (reprinted by Alan Sutton Publishing) recorded every person in the county capable of bearing arms in 1608.

46

It needed a tall man to manage these 18-foot pikes. The pikes were of ash wood and pikemen wore strong leather gauntlets to protect their hands from splinters.

In Sapperton in the year 1608, out of 33 able-bodied men, 24 worked for Sir Henry Poole.

FITT TO SERVE WITH A CALYVER

PYKEMAN

MUSKETYER

The name CALYVER refers to a gun similar to a musket, but lighter in weight, being about 12 pounds and so needing no forked resting stick.

These men were independently employed in 1608

2 Musketyer :-

William Walter Milner	William Halle Husbandman

→

+ 1

George Bridges Smith (no detail size)

?

3 Pykemen :-

Richard Longford Husbandman	Walter Longford Husbandman	Henry Wood Carpenter

↓

The 1608 census page from one of the school's scrapbooks, displayed in Cirencester Library as part of an exhibition at the time of the last national census.

3 to serve with a Calyver :-

Thomas Halle Husbandman	Nicholas Halle Husbandman	Edward Hill Taylor

→

These twenty-four men worked for Sir Henry in 1608

8 Pykemen:

Richard Collor
Servant

Michaell Clevinger
Servant

John Ducke
Servant

William Winstone
Husbandman

William Teynton
Husbandman

* Reginald Legge
Husbandman

John Hunt
Husbandman

William Hiet
Servant

7 Musketyer:

Edward Rogers
Servant

Thomas Kendal
Servant

Gyles Lawrence
Servant

John Poole
Servant

Richard Stephens
Servant

Edward Webbe
Servant

Thomas Wilson
Husbandman

* This man's surname
seems the only
surname to survive
from the 1327
Subsidy Rolls.

to serve with Calyver :- 9

Thomas Damsell Servant	Robert Perren Servant	Thomas Bushopp Husbandman
Michaell Damsell Servant	Richard Sellinger Servant	William English Husbandman
Mathewe Poole Servant	Leonard Watson Husbandman	John Nelmes Husbandman

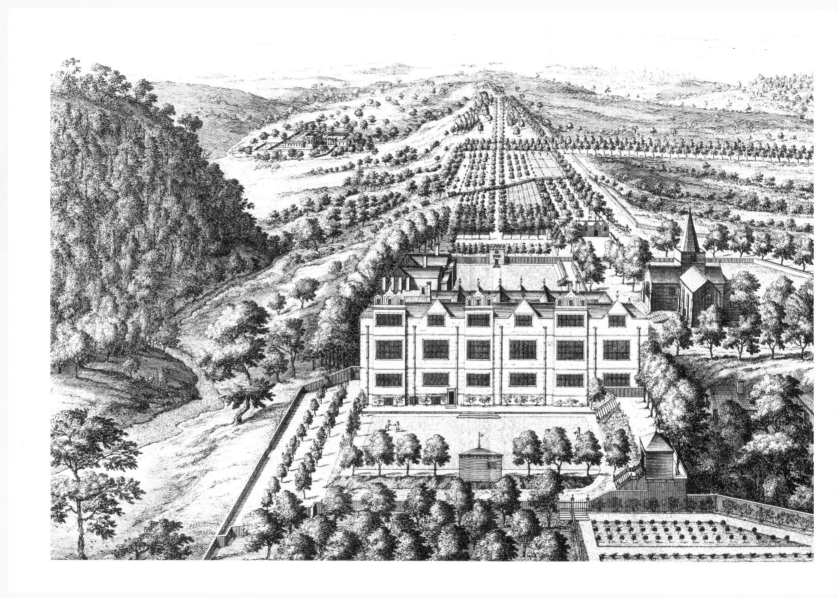

SAPPERTON HOUSE

Sir Henry Poole now lies in Sapperton Church and his house is no more.

So where did he live, this chief employer of Sapperton men in 1608?

Important enough to have twice been High Sheriff of Gloucestershire and M.P. for Cirencester, where is his great house now?

We are fortunate that our own local historian, Sir Robert Atkyns, produced a history of Gloucestershire in 1707 which was accompanied by a volume of illustrations of the great houses in the county, and he included this picture of Sapperton House in it.

The Victoria History dates it as "probably built in the earlier part of the previous (17th) century" which lets us suppose that it may have been built in the later years of this Sir Henry's life. He died in 1616.

So many questions remain unanswered, though we are searching for answers all the time. Was it built on the site of a previous house? Where did the Lords of the Manor live before? Today no trace remains (except for a few piles of rubble near the church stile, and the terraced edge of the main lawn as it drops sharply down on the north side of the field) so we find it hard to imagine, when standing on the site, what a centre of bustling splendour it must have been three and a half centuries ago.

Two major source books. The relevant volume of the ongoing *Victoria History of the Counties of England*, published by Oxford University Press, and central to most reference libraries; and Sir Robert Atkyns' *The Ancient & Present State of Glostershire*, an 18th-century county history, reprinted in facsimile by EP Publishing. Both supplied much in the way of detailed information on Sapperton.

Sir Henry Poole died in 1616 and his canopied tomb in the north transept is one of the gems of Sapperton Church. The well-known series of "Observer" books gives the tomb a full-page picture in its volume on "British Architecture". Sir Henry, his wife and his children can be seen on and around this interesting marble monument.

At the right-hand side of the tomb, a small negro head is mounted on the wall and we puzzled over its significance. We wondered if the family had links with the West Indies, or was he a favoured servant? Then, a friend interested in heraldry thought the ribbon-wrapped bar below the head suggested it was a 'device' brought back from the Crusades to be used somewhere on the owner's armour.

The interesting Jacobean carvings at the pew ends in the church came from the Pooles' house when the church was extensively remodelled in the early 18th century.

This is the site of Sapperton House today, looking across the front lawn.
From this field the early 17th-century Poole family would have had a good view of their near neighbours, the Hancox farmers of Daneway House.
This often bleak spot, overlooking the Chalford valley, must have been the focal point of feverish activity during the decades before and after the death of Sir Henry in 1616. On this site a great house was being built (or vastly re-modelled?) while across the valley, at Daneway, the High Building would soon be added to the existing 13th-century structure.
As with the death of Sir Henry an era ended, so at Daneway, the lives of two of its principal characters were coming to a close.

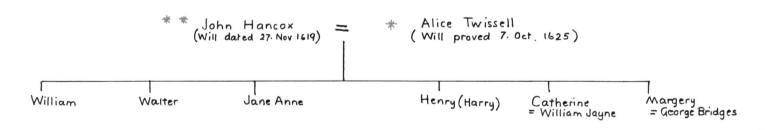

* * John Hancox
(Will dated 27. Nov 1619)
= * Alice Twissell
(Will proved 7. Oct. 1625)

William   Walter   Jane Anne   Henry (Harry)   Catherine
= William Jayne   Margery
= George Bridges

<u>Will of John Hancock</u> — Proved at Gloucester 25. March 1619/20

In the name of God Amen, the XXVII day of November 1619, I John Hancock of Denway in the parish of Bysley in the Countye of Gloucester, Yeoman, being weeke of body but in good and perfect remembrance do make my will in manner and form following– I desire to be buried in the Church or Churchyard of Bysley.

All my landes which I have at Litteridge called by the name of north Ekins I give unto my son Walter Hancocks and to his heyres, but not to have it so long as my wife doth live and keeps herself widow. That part which I have in Hillhouse which is halfe I do give to my son William Hancocke paying unto my daughter Jane Hancock forty poundes. I doe also give unto my daughter Jane ten pounds to be payed unto her at my decease. Unto my daughter Ann Hancocks three score powndes and to stay for it Two yeares affter my decease and then to have Thirty Powndes at the two yeares ends, and the other Thirty pownds at the end of the next year following. Unto my sonne William two oxen and two horses and all manner of plow Implements after the decease of my wife. Unto my Sonn William the table boardes in the halls and their appurtenances and one cheste, one chayre, one press, one bedsteede, one bed with all that belongs to it. Unto my Sonn Henry Hancock one oxe, one cowe, one horse on the decease of my wife. Unto my son Walter one bedsteede and one bed. Unto my daughter Katheren Joan two sheepe. Unto my daughter Margery Bridges two sheepe. Unto my servant Robert Nobell one sheepe. Unto William Martin 3s. 4d. I do appoint all the armourie or furniture which I do stand charged with all my wife shall leave it to my sonne William. I do give the lease of this my living called Denway Farm unto my son William Hancock and to enter it upon decease of my wife.

(We are indebted to Lady Denny of Daneway House for this information)

Sapperton children with Lady Denny, about to visit the inscribed tree in Daneway Woods (see page 62). Much of the detail relating to Daneway in the pages which follow owes its origin to Lady Denny or to the history of the house which she and her husband compiled for an open day.

* Will of Alice Hancoxe – Proved at Gloucester 7. October 1625

The Eleventh Day of Julye 1625, I Alse Hancoxe of Deanways in the parishe of Byslye and County of Glouc.' wyddow, being sycke in body but of perfect memory doe make this my last will and Testament in manner following — I desire to be buryed in the parishe Church or Churchyarde of Bysley. I give unto Walter Hancoxe my Sonne one Cowe, six sheepe, the best cardering save one, Three pieces of pewter, eyght Bushells of bareley, one black coulte, one halfe of the best brass pan, the Ten acres of Corne of barley and oates that I rented of Mr. Freeme, hee paying the rent for the lands and three poundes in monye. Unto my daughter Margery Brydges one Heyfer of one yeare and twenty shillings in money, my wedding Ring and the best brass pann. Unto Georg Bridges my Sonn in Lawe one peece of goulde of two and twenty shillings and two sheepe. Unto my daughter Jane tenn pounds in money within one year after my decease, three pieces of pewter, half the lynnen, one pott, one Couldron, one pan, one peece of medlye Clothe to make her a Gownde, one Bedd, yf she have the best Bedd then she is to have the worst Cov'rlett, and eight sheepe. Unto Annis my daughter one Bedd, one pott, one pann, half the linnen, six peeces of pewter one Coffer wch stoode at the stayre heade, one calfe that I bought of her. Unto Catherin Jayne my daughter one heyfer of one yeere ould, one payre of Tacke hookes and one peece of goulde of 5s. Unto my sonn in law Willia' Jayne two and twenty shillings in goulde and the sayde sonn in lawes child Willia' Jayne one heyfer one year old and a half, two sheepe and to his son Harry Jeyne two sheepe and one calfe. Unto my sonn Harrye Hancoxe two children, a silver spoone and to my daughter Catherin the beste ——— unto my sonn Willia' one cubborde in the haule, one halfe of the best pann, the best pott and the longe coffer and the best Cauldren. Unto my sonn Henry Hancoxe one cowe, one pott, one brass pann, the smallest saveing one, one bedd, and all things that doth belong to him, and one coffer. Unto my sister Margrett Haukins a Noble yearely during her lyfe toward her mayntenance. Unto Joan Harbert my god daughter one Aperne, one Carcheife and a platter, and I ordain my two sonnes Willia' Hancoxe and Henry Hancoxe to be my executors of this my last Will and Testament. And I make my son in lawes Georg Brydges and Willia' Jayne to be my overseers and I geve them tenn groats a peece.
Witnesses — John Harbert, George Bridges — his mark.

56

As we read these two wills, John and Alice become real people to us. Especially Alice, who so thoughtfully shares out all her earthly possessions among her offspring in minute detail.
These items, probably very well-used, suggest a spartan way of life at Daneway, dominated by this frugal housewife, her closely-knit family revolving round her.

This picture of the inner hall at Daneway House has, on its extreme left edge, 'the ogee trefoil-arched entrance (to the oratory) typical of the date 1339.' So, this could well be where "one cubborde in the haule" stood which William was bequeathed.
He now becomes the 'leading light' in the Daneway drama.

THE MANOR OF SAPPERTON ABOUT 1642

Years pass and the storm clouds of the Civil War gather over this peaceful valley, as the Royalist Pooles overlook the farm and home of yeoman William Hancocks, Captain-to-be in Cromwell's Army.

Cloth manufacturers of Stroud and Cirencester were united in their condemnation of the King's trade policy which they felt

gave unfair advantage to Dutch wool merchants. Our neighbouring village of Frampton Mansell, too, had anti-Royalist tendencies. The close proximity of these warring factions must have led to much ill-will, setting friend against friend, even father against son.

We are grateful to "Cirencester Newspaper Co" for permission to use this photograph taken when the "King's Army of the West" enacted Civil War skirmishes near Daneway in 1973.

60

As we study William Hancocks (or Hancox) we conclude he must have been a man of strong character, as had been many of his family before him.

When you consider these yeomen farmers, living in the shadow of the feudal estate of Sapperton, ever maintaining their independence at a time when most of their neighbours were 'bending their knee' to the great house in Sapperton, you cannot but admire their dogged, enduring pride.

[In 1603 Robert Hancox had bought Daneway from Giles Godrington, but the Hancoxes had already been living there for 200 years, leasing the house. Their tenure was to continue for 457 years until the death of John Hancox in 1860.]

Deep in Daneway woods stood this remarkable tree. We photographed it before
it blew down in the winter of 1983. William Hancox had carved on it all those years
ago "HIS WOOD / WILLIAM HANCOX / CAPTAIN IN / O. CROMWEL /
ARMY / 16 ." It was deteriorating but Tom Denny could recall its clearer days.
Apparently it was traditional for Hancox heirs to inscribe a tree during their
lifetime and several such trees are around, but this was the oldest.

These troubled days must have seen many skirmishes similar to this, (enacted at Daneway 1973). In July 1644, when Charles was marching through the Cotswolds to the West in pursuit of Essex, he spent one night at Sapperton as the guest of the Pooles. When he was finally defeated in 1649, then the reckoning came for Sapperton....

During the war, a committee of Parliament, sitting in London, valued country estates and decided how much each could afford to "furnish the sinews of war." On 28·July·1644 they assessed Sir William Poole's forced loan at £1,500. It seems he did not pay, for on 29·July·1646, an order went out for him to be brought into custody.

Sir William pleaded that both he and his father had been compelled to comply with the King's party whilst they prevailed in their county. In spite of this plea (which was probably not true of his father, Sir Henry, who was a Royalist anyway) the commissioners for the county were there upon directed to seize and secure his estate.

Being unable to discharge his debt he borrowed money from Gabriel Beck of Lincoln's Inn before his death in 1651. Then most of his land was mortgaged and the mortgagees sold the Manor of Sapperton to Sir Robert Atkyns in 1661 to pay off that debt, and a new era began in Sapperton.

Bristol and Gloucestershire Archaeological Society Transactions, Volume 50 (1928). One of many such county archaeological and historical society journals existing in Britain, promoting the local study and publication of history and archaeology. An article in the 1928 volume furnished valuable details on the transition from Sir William Poole to Sir Robert Atkyns in Sapperton.

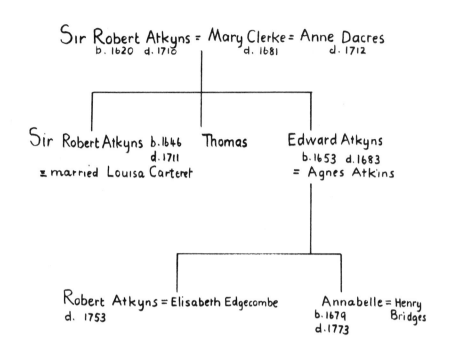

Sir Robert Atkyns = Mary Clerke = Anne Dacres
b. 1620 d. 1710   d. 1681   d. 1712

Sir Robert Atkyns b.1646   Thomas   Edward Atkyns
              d.1711   b. 1653 d.1683
= married Louisa Carteret   = Agnes Atkins

Robert Atkyns = Elisabeth Edgecombe   Annabelle = Henry
d. 1753   b.1679   Bridges
                                             d.1773

Sir Robert Atkyns bought most of the manor of
Sapperton in 1661 and added to it in 1667. This
Sir Robert (whom we call "the Elder") was a Judge.
He must have been very fair for someone wrote, "He
is an honest judge in an age of rascals." He had three
children. One of them, Sir Robert (the Younger), pictured here, became famous as the
author of the first printed history of Gloucestershire.

Sir Robert (the Younger) was also a Judge and M.P. for Cirencester but is chiefly remembered for two other things.

First, he achieved fame as the author of "The Ancient and Present State of Gloucestershire", which he did not have the pleasure of seeing completed as it was not published until 1712, a year after his death.

Secondly, he will be remembered by visitors to the south transept of our church, where his effigy reclines upon its elbow in a most dignified manner.

He died in 1711, of dysentery in London, without heir, and left Sapperton House to his niece, Annabella.

He had not lived there himself for some years, having moved out of his father's home to Pinbury Park nearby, where he devoted most of his time to writing his history book.

NEWSFLASH

Wilts & Glos. Standard.

9.9.1985

Exciting finds in Sapperton Church

A burial chamber, undiscovered for more than two and a half centuries has just been found during recent restoration work on the monument of Sir Robert Atkyns in Sapperton parish church.

Sir Robert Atkyns, a famous county historian and author of the "Present and Ancient State of Gloucestershire" died in 1711 and a large monument was erected to him and his wife in the church of St. Kenelm at Sapperton.

During recent restoration work on the monument, Mr. Richard Marsh, a member of the Wells Cathedral Restoration team, discovered the burial chamber under the floor of the south transept of the church where the monument stands.

Hidden under stone flags since 1716, when Lady Atkyns was buried, a flight of stone steps lead down to a rectangular, arched, burial chamber, containing the lead-lined coffins of Sir Robert and his wife.

Now that the chamber has been discovered plans are underway to carry out a full investigation.

Sir Anthony Denny, chairman of the Monuments Committee, Mr. Christopher Bishop, the church architect, and Mr. Richard Marsh will be conferring with archaeological and restoration experts from London very soon.

Until the investigation is complete no arrangements are being made for visitors.

Conservator Roger Harris leads the way in !

Yesterday Miss Pinnell went down into the vault that has just been discoverd about three weeks ago. No one knew it was there except the mason who moved a flag stone and saw eight steps going down. The village was very excited but no body was allowed in the church.

Chris. (7)

67

On Sept. 26 1985 Miss
Pinnell was allowed to
go down to the vault
under Sir Robert Atkyns
Memorial to take
photographs. Men found
it while investigating
damp. Only one flag
stone could be moved
so it was a tight
squeeze to get down
the steps. The candles
used in 1711 and
1716 had made

sooty marks on the arched ceiling. The two coffins
were on the floor. When Miss Pinnell got down
she could see that lots of small stones had
fallen on Lady Atkyns coffin and broken it.
She was sad about this.   Fenn (8)

There are many things which puzzle us about this vault. There has been no fall from the roof of the chamber, so where has all the soil and rubble come from that lies on top of the two Atkyns' coffins? The wood lying around seems too much to have come from the Atkyns coffins alone, and why did we find it all in such a muddle?

Sir Robert and Lady Atkyns lie in lead-lined coffins because it was the rule that only such lined coffins could be buried within the Church walls for reasons of hygiene.

The conservator, Roger Harris, said he was interested that some of the mortar used in the walls (pre-Portland type cement) still had not hardened after two and a half centuries!

Roger Harris kindly gave us this photograph which he had taken of the nameplate on Sir Robert's coffin.

Oct 10·1985. The mystery deepens! An expert, Julian W. S. Litten, from the Victoria & Albert Museum, has been called in to look at our vault. In his opinion there are not two coffins there, but five. The extra three, placed on top of the Atkyns' ones, have so disintegrated that little remains. Even the bones have gone to white powder. Who they were is still a mystery as the iron nameplates were too corroded to read.

Dear Pat Pinnell

SAPPERTON ST KENELM: ATKYNS VAULT

Thank you for your letter of 12 November. Of course you may quote me in your forthcoming book regarding the Atkyns vault. The details are as follows:-

The vault is situated centrally beneath the the south transept and measures 2.45m N-S and 2.61m E-W and is constructed of blocks of oolitic limestone; it is entered via a flight of eight steps, also of oolitic limestone, from the north. There are five coffins in the vault, all on an E-W axis, head to the W. The two earlier coffins (lead-lapped inner wooden shells, the outer velvet covered shells having disintegrated) contain, to the North, the remains of Sir Robert Atkyns (d.1711) and, to the South, Lady Louise Atkyns (d.1716). The three remaining coffins are single-shell constructions of the first quarter of the 19th century of the type associated with earth burial; one rests on the floor between the earlier lead shells whilst the other two (being in an advanced state of decay and having collapsed inside one another) rest on top of that of Lady Louise Atkyns. At some stage after the deposit of the single-shell wooden coffins soil was introduced, probably as a sanitary precaution arising from the use of single-shell coffins. None of the contents of the later coffins was identifiable, the stamped iron breastplates having corroded.

Why these later coffins were put in the vault remains a mystery; the obvious explanation seems that someone knew of the vault's existence and that it had not been used since 1716 and, assuming that there was extra room he/she chose to take it over for the use of their family. Sadly, they were not au fait with undertaking techniques associated with vault burial; had they been so then the coffins would have emulated those of the Atkyns'. The most probable candidate for such a take-over would be either an incumbent or a churchwarden.

I hope that there are enough details here to give you a picture of what the vault was like and what its contents can tell us.

Yours sincerely,

Julian W S Litten
Department of Prints & Drawings.

One of the national museums is sometimes called in to advise on a major historical discovery and to analyse material which comes to light. Most of these will also attempt to identify relevant artefacts and provide a research facility for interested members of the public.

Sir Robert Atkyns, the
Sapperton historian, wrote
the first history of Gloucestershire.
Here, in our church, we feel
very near to our famous
ancestors. We wonder if Sir
Robert is watching all this
work on his memorial in the church.
Does the disorder in his last
resting place cause him annoyance?
Take heart, Sir Robert, your
trials will soon be over.
Tomorrow, Oct 24, 1985, the
Conservator working on your tomb
will close the vault and you will
be left in peace again.

1730 saw the end of Sapperton House. Why? We are not sure. In 1711 Annabella inherited it, selling it in 1730 to the first Lord Bathurst. The present Earl Bathurst told us he thought a fire occurred soon after the sale. Some of the woodwork was removed and used in the Church and much of the stone taken to the centre of Oakley Park to build picturesque "Alfred's Hall".

We sometimes picnic near the ruin in the wood, known
as "Alfred's Hall".
The first Lord Bathurst, who died in 1775 at the age of
ninety, enjoyed re-shaping his estate, especially that
lying west of his home, between Cirencester and Sapperton,
and this 'ruin' was part of his landscaping plan.
Each time we enter the woods near Park Corner we remember
this energetic nobleman, friend of writers and poets, who
changed the face of our countryside as he cut away hills and
laid down avenues and rides for five miles through the
Park and Oakley Wood to Sapperton.

The first Lord Bathurst had another dream, as told in
this letter from Alexander Pope, the poet, to his friend Digby...

1722.

"I am told... that Mrs. Mary Digby talks... of seeing my Lord Bathurst's wood... How I wish to be her guide through that enchanted forest... I look upon myself as the magician appropriated to the place, without whom no mortal can penetrate into the recesses of those sacred shades. I could pass whole days in only describing to her the future, and as yet visionary beauties that are to rise in those scenes; the palace that is to be built, the pavilions that are to glitter, the colonnades that are to adorn them. Nay, more, the meeting of the Thames and Severn, which (when the noble owner has finer dreams than ordinary) are to be led into each other's embraces through secret caverns of not above twelve or fifteen miles, till they rise and celebrate their marriage in the midst of an immense amphitheatre, which is to be the admiration of posterity a hundred years hence."

Herbert Evans' *Highways and Byways in Oxford and the Cotswolds* (1905) which quotes Pope's letter to Digby. The turn of the century was rich in such books which, although not always accurate, assemble an extraordinary array of local and historical detail.

75

His dream was shared by others.
Here, at the Swan Inn, Stroud, the
Committee met with the wily
tunnel contractor, Charles Jones.

But the dream, for some, ended
here, in Sapperton Churchyard
There were many more burials
here in the canal-building years.

It depended on 'navvies' like this
to move tons of earth each day
with only a spade, wheel-barrow
and pick-axe...

... as they cut a canal along the
Stroud/Chalford valley (and built
28 locks to raise it to the
Daneway Basin.)

Gloucester Docks and the Sharpness Canal
gave Sapperton School the opportunity
to experience a canal from a real
narrow boat.

Moira Gobey, the school cook, was able to give a first-hand account of life centred on the canal. She had lived in the house beside the entrance to the canal tunnel since 1934 and her grandfather had been a canal employee since the early 1920s.

TUNNEL MOUTH SAPPERTON

When the Canal reached Daneway it could not go round or over the Hill, it had to go through.........................

(Photograph, taken around 1900, by kind permission of The Record Office, Gloucester.)

Robert Whitworth was one of the best surveyors of that time, and in August 1783 he began work, marking the line of the Sapperton Tunnel, sighting by means of tall poles in trees. For this important task he received £93. 7s. 6d.

Alas, he was unable to ascertain the geology of the area deep below the line he selected. Charles Jones, who got the contract to cut out the tunnel, met many difficulties when he came to rock harder than he had anticipated. He drilled these 24 shafts first.

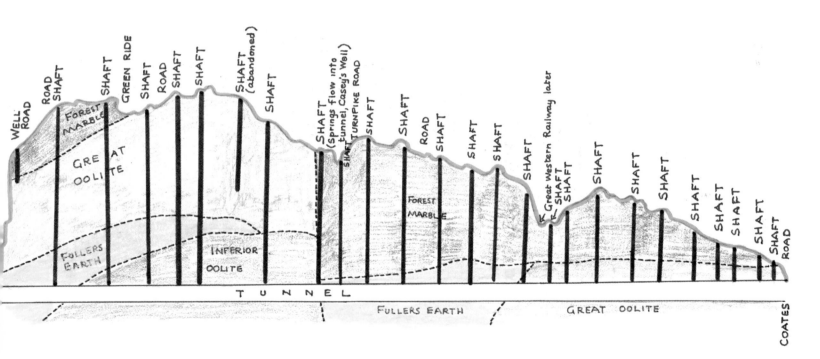

LET US PRETEND WE CAN CUT THROUGH THE GROUND TO SEE INSIDE THE SAPPERTON TUNNEL:

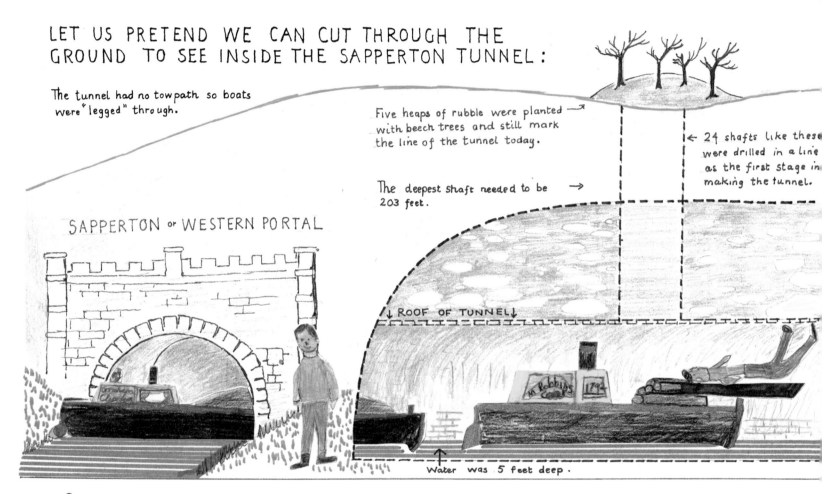

The tunnel had no towpath so boats were "legged" through.

Five heaps of rubble were planted with beech trees and still mark the line of the tunnel today.

← 24 shafts like these were drilled in a line as the first stage in making the tunnel.

The deepest shaft needed to be 203 feet. →

SAPPERTON or WESTERN PORTAL

↓ ROOF OF TUNNEL ↓

Mr Robbins Coates 1793

Water was 5 feet deep.

Boats went through the tunnel in single file. For part of the day priority was given to those waiting in Daneway Basin and at a decided time the traffic flow changed and those who had been waiting at the Coates end entered by the Eastern Portal.

Usually each boat had 2 "leggers", one on each side. We think our leggers legs are too high as they 'walked' along the sides rather than the roof of the tunnel. Leggers would wait in "The Bricklayers Arms" or "Tunnel House" to be hired. They "legged" about one mile per hour.

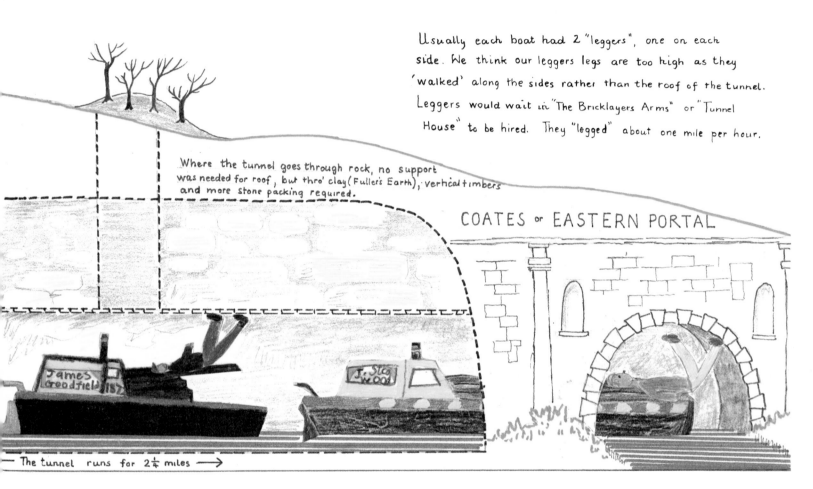

Where the tunnel goes through rock, no support was needed for roof, but thro' clay (Fuller's Earth), vertical timbers and more stone packing required.

COATES or EASTERN PORTAL

James Goodfield 187_

J. Sto W OO

← The tunnel runs for 2¼ miles →

Our tunnel was the highest part (the "Summit") of the whole canal system linking the Severn to the Thames. Always it was difficult to keep enough water in this part to float boats. The clay lining often cracked and when the water leaked out the canal had to be closed for repairs.

Bruce Carter's *Gunpowder Tunnel* (Hamish Hamilton, 1955) and John Poole's *Saul Adam* (Thornhill Press, 1973). Two stories read by the school to help to capture the atmosphere of the canal in its heyday. One based on the building of the tunnel and the other on and around the canal.

Many bricks were used in the construction of the canal and tunnel. This inn, now called "The Daneway Inn" was originally "The Bricklayers Arms." It was first used by the navvies, then the bargees as they waited with their boats to use the Tunnel. Leggers too, waited here to be hired.

But the Tunnel was not built without human cost! A study of the Parish Records of Coates and Sapperton shows that during the tunnel-building years of 1784 to 1788 almost double the number of burials took place.

" The Gloucester Journal " of January 22 nd 1787 reported :
" ... In the prosecution of this work, many men have lost their lives; one man was killed a few days ago by the carelessness of his companion, who suffered one of the boxes used in drawing the earth up the shafts, to fall down into the pit, which killed the person at the bottom. " (His brother!)

On July 19th, 1788, King George III inspected the nearly completed tunnel and in April 1789 the first boat passed through.

The tunnel was 3,817 yards in length, 15 feet in width and 15 feet in height. Robert Whitworth's estimated cost of £36,575 had been considerably exceeded.

At its completion the tunnel was hailed as an outstanding feat of engineering and the canal's most prosperous time came during the early 19th century, peaking in 1840-1842 with an income of £11,000 in 1841.

However, in 1841-45 the G.W.R. line was opened to Gloucester and canal receipts dropped to £3,000 in 1855.

rom 1784 till 1789, while the Tunnel was being constructed, this, the Daneway Wharf asin, would have been the centre of great activity Here, near "The Bricklayers Arms,"

e barges would
ve waited to
ter the Tunnel
hich goes into
e hill about
quarter of a
ile from these
uildings, photographed
1906.
rough the bridge
es the last of
e 28 locks
ming up from
troud, the Summit
ock, and then the

anal curves to the right towards the Daneway Portal (the Sapperton entrance of the unnel.) We are grateful to David Viner, Curator, Corinium Museum, Cirencester for
this photograph.

Today, much of the Canal lies in ruins.

Here you see Stroud Sea Cadets, with an officer, lifting fallen stonework at the Daneway Portal, prior to restoration by the Stroudwater-Thames & Severn Canal Trust, a voluntary group whose aim is to get the canal back into working order. This Trust holds a sponsored Canal Walk each year (usually in May) involving local organisations and schools.

This event provides much of their finance. So far they have dredged lengths of canal and rebuilt lock chambers and the Coates Portal but their greatest challenge lies ahead when they consider the Tunnel itself.

Sapperton children taking part in the Canal Walk complete the fourteen mile course.

In 1982, when these pictures were taken, they entered it by boat to survey its condition, but it has not really been navigable since 1927. (Pictures kindly provided by David Boakes, Framilode Productions).

Stroud Teachers' Centre proved another good searching ground, in this case assisting with material from their 'canal box'.

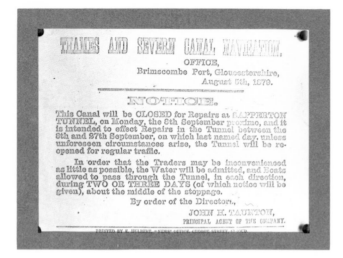

THAMES AND SEVERN CANAL NAVIGATION.

OFFICE,
Brimscombe Port, Gloucestershire,
August 5th, 1879.

NOTICE.

This Canal will be CLOSED for Repairs at SAPPERTON TUNNEL, on Monday, the 8th September proximo, and it is intended to effect Repairs in the Tunnel between the 8th and 27th September, on which last named day, unless unforeseen circumstances arise, the Tunnel will be re-opened for regular traffic.

In order that the Traders may be inconvenienced as little as possible, the Water will be admitted, and Boats allowed to pass through the Tunnel, in each direction, during TWO OR THREE DAYS (of which notice will be given), about the middle of the stoppage.

By order of the Directors,

JOHN H. TAUNTON,
PRINCIPAL AGENT OF THE COMPANY.

PRINTED BY E. HULBERT, "NEWS" OFFICE, GEORGE STREET, STROUD.

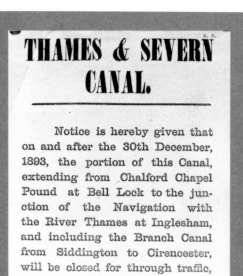

THAMES & SEVERN CANAL.

Notice is hereby given that on and after the 30th December, 1893, the portion of this Canal, extending from Chalford Chapel Pound at Bell Lock to the junction of the Navigation with the River Thames at Inglesham, and including the Branch Canal from Siddington to Cirencester, will be closed for through traffic, until further notice.

BY ORDER.

J. MAHON,
Clerk to the Company.

Paddington, London, 28th December, 1893.

Two things brought about the closure of our canal. There was a great shortage of water in these upper reaches. Evaporation in summer and cracks in the clay "puddling" made the water level drop so much that boats could not float along, then the canal would be closed for repairs. Merchants, demanding more reliability, supported the developing railway.

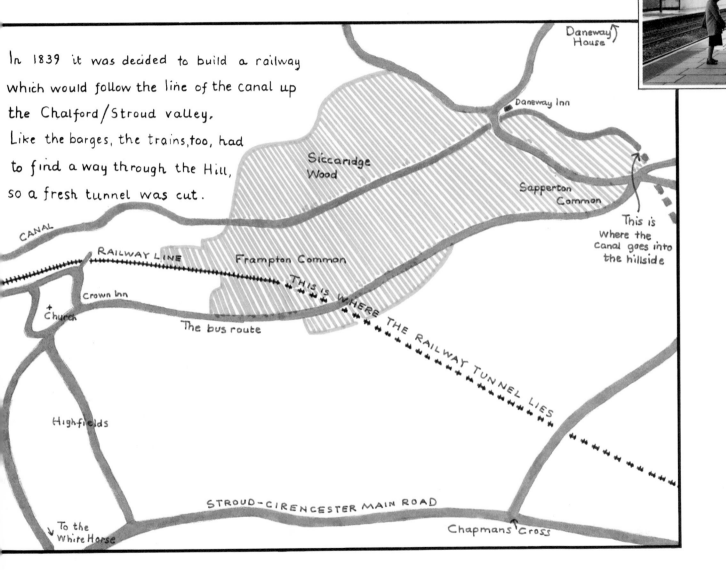

In 1839 it was decided to build a railway
which would follow the line of the canal up
the Chalford/Stroud valley.
Like the barges, the trains, too, had
to find a way through the Hill,
so a fresh tunnel was cut.

A school group travel from Stroud to Swindon by train to see their valley from the railway.

Footbridge

Daneway House

Daneway Inn

Siccaridge Wood

Sapperton Common

This is where the canal goes into the hillside

CANAL

RAILWAY LINE

Frampton Common

THIS IS WHERE THE RAILWAY TUNNEL LIES

Crown Inn

Church

The bus route

Highfields

STROUD-CIRENCESTER MAIN ROAD

Chapmans Cross

To the White Horse

89

In front of the *North Star* at Swindon's Great Western Railway Museum – a trip to see the kind of locomotives which were running in the early days of steam.

Once more the roar of gunpowder could be heard beneath the feet of Sappertonians as they walked on the Frampton Mansell road, while a new generation of navvies 'moled' their way through our hill.
Some of these navvies were housed in "The Barracks" which was then a terraced row of cottages ¼ mile west of Sapperton village (but extensively altered 1971).
The new railway tunnel was officially opened on Whit Monday, May 12th, 1845, completed by the G.W.R.

After that, the roar of gunpowder was replaced by the roar of the latest model in steam locomotives!

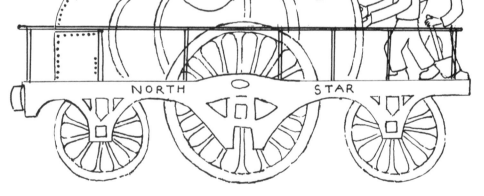

NORTH STAR

90

Mr. Parker a local retired railwayman who had lived through the great days of the GWR was able to describe them from his own experience.

Since 1845 how many generations of
young Sappertonians must have "train-
spotted" from the banks of this cutting
where Green Lane meets the Stroud to
Cirencester Road?
It is much safer to watch the trains
emerging from the tunnel here than at
the other end in the Frampton Mansell woods...

... even though, there, a modern
telephone has been installed by
the Railway Authorities to ensure
the safety of those who need to
cross the line with cows or tractors.

A Voice from the Past . . . .

We were extremely fortunate to obtain the following reminiscences of a 90 year-old lady (Great Aunt Sarah), whose family lived in Coates and Sapperton at the time of the opening of the Railway. She wrote them in 1939 and they provide fascinating links with the navvies and the first school-master to teach in Sapperton School as we know it today.
We are indebted to her great niece Miss Brenda Matthews who gave them to us, knowing that Thomas Matthews (b. 1804), her great grandfather had been a schoolmaster here around 1848-1850.

Extract from "A Brief Sketch of the Life of My Father, Thomas Matthews, Born 19th November 1804 Died 25th November 1860. Buried at Sapperton.

"After his marriage he worked at Mr. Silk's factory until it closed down... and then came to Coates. How my father got started on that part of his career I cannot say, but he was always keen on books and education and also given to good works, and in some way got in touch with a Mr. Dent who lived in Yorkshire but had some model cottages in Coates - they are still there - a long row of semi-detached cottages as you enter the village standing well back from the road. Mr. Dent was, I believe, connected in some way with a rich and philanthropic lady of Cheltenham and... with Quakers....I think these good people got my father to take on the school at Coates as a sort of missionary effort, for the place was at a very low ebb with a parson who hunted foxes rather than souls! and utter ignorance seemed to prevail in the village but not vice. My parents found the people simple and kindly but steeped in ignorance and indifference to all, what you may term, higher influence.
But in the seven years of my parents' residence there came a great change. Father kept school and taught the children a good deal more than is contained in any syllabus! Had short services for the elders weekdays, got them to Church Sundays, had service outdoors for the navvies who were making the Great Western Railway. My brothers Henry and Tom used to tell how they had to go and hold the lantern for Father to read the Bible, and to help in the singing. Mother helped loyally despite the cares of a young family - taught the women to cut out and sew and to keep their babies clean and wholesome...

...In short, my dear parents looked after their bodies and souls and worked wonders, and as long as they lived were loved and gratefully remembered by Coates folk. Our family occupied one of the cottages I mentioned. They had good kitchens and sculleries and I suppose three bedrooms.

My father's fame as a schoolmaster and a good man had grown and he was invited to Sapperton and accepted the appointment, but who the authorities were I do not know, nor where the salary came from, over and above the pupils' weekly pence.

School House, Sapperton

Here he had more scope – good school accommodation for those days and a good house. The scholars too were many of them of a different class – all the neighbouring farmers sent their children – some from a distance brought their dinner – and we had two weekly boarders I know at one period – Mary West of Oaksey and a boy named Owen Cordy. Mother's life must have been one of ceaseless toil with her large family.

She took the girls for afternoon school, teaching them needlework, sewing, knitting and cutting out. Father was always enlarging his own borders! Taught himself a certain amount of French (I have his beautifully bound French Testament now). Also land surveying, and so was often land measuring for the farmers, taking his own boys and some of the other lads to help and thereby teaching them too! "

(The family moved back into Cirencester in 1853 when Thomas entered employment with the Bathursts.)

In 1848 a new building for the school was given to the village by Lord Bathurst. Where the children went before this we do not know, but in 1847 there were 75 children attending school somewhere! Sir Robert Atkyns (d. 1711) had left 2 annuities of £3 each for "teaching poor children to read, say the catechism and to fit them for their work."

We do not think our school today has changed much externally 'though the two small porches were probably added years later. It must have been a bit crowded by 1851 for the Census mentioned 82 scholars at that time and 55 children under school age.

We tried to imagine the hard lives of some of those early pupils.

This 1906 photograph of Group 3, Sapperton School, was kindly provided by Miss H. Allen. The clothes and hairstyles of children and teachers interested us. Their expressions too, seemed to suggest that this was a serious business.

One of the best sources of material proved to be the villagers themselves. Here the school sifts through photographs at 'The Barracks', the old lodgings of the railway navvies.

This photograph, provided by Mr. Bush of Beacon Farm, could portray mothers who worked on that farm around 1906.

The Sapperton Craftsmen

At the beginning of the 20th century a new group of names appears on the Sapperton scene. The Barnsley brothers, Ernest and Sydney, with Ernest Gimson, made this village the centre of their craft workshops for the production of beautiful and simple furniture, inspired by the tradition of William Morris.

Moving from nearby Pinbury Park, they came to Sapperton, building houses for themselves on land given them by Lord Bathurst, and using Daneway House to display their furniture in a suitable setting.

Photograph and names supplied by Miss Jewson, daughter of Norman Jewson

Mr. and Mrs. Herbert Barnsley , E. Corfield , Ernest & Alice Barnsley
Uncle Will   Gertrude Corfield , Auntie Lucy , Mrs. Will (Clara)
        Uncle Sidney

<u>Some of the Sapperton Craftsmen at Upper Dorvel House, Sapperton, 1906</u>

In August 1907, Norman Jewson, a young architect, walked to Sapperton through Cirencester Park. He had heard of the Sapperton Craftsmen and when he met them he found his ideas matched theirs, so he decided to stay and work with them.

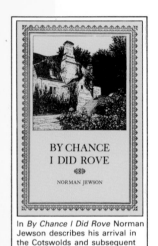

BY CHANCE
I DID ROVE

NORMAN JEWSON

In *By Chance I Did Rove* Norman Jewson describes his arrival in the Cotswolds and subsequent close association with Ernest Gimson and the Barnsleys.

In 1911 he married Mary Barnsley, daughter of Ernest Barnsley. Their daughter, Miss Nancy Jewson kindly provided us with this picture of her parents' wedding. Mr Jewson and his family lived at Batchelor's Court, Sapperton.

There is a great revival of interest in the group's achievements and many people come here specially to see their homes and the houses they designed.

Miss Jewson, pictured here, has recently moved from this, her life-long home.

<u>After a visit, one of the Juniors wrote</u>:

"About half an hour ago Miss Jewson came to talk about her father. He was friends with Mr. Gimson and the Barnsleys. In 1894 Gimson and the Barnsleys moved into Pinbury Park. They done it up real nice. So Lord Bathurst wanted it back. He made a deal with the three friends. He said they could each choose a piece of land on his estate and build their own houses and he would pay for them.

Mr. Gimson had Leasowes, E. Barnsley had Upper Dorvel House and Sidney Barnsley had Beechanger.

On Sunday night a milkboy saw a fire. It was coming from Leasowes. He rose the alarm and all the villagers came out of church. They all ran to the house. It took them twenty minutes to get all the things out. They even got the grand piano. When the firemen came they had to go down to the valley to get the water.

Before the fire it was thatched. After the fire they put tiles on the roof. Later Miss Jewson took us to her cottage and showed us some of her things. She showed us a plaster mould with her mothers initials in it. Mr Gimson is famous for his ceilings.

We hope to go and see one at Upper Dorvel House." 　　　　　— Sharon (11)

Sir Anthony and Lady Denny held a special exhibition at Daneway House.
They had a 1904 catalogue with pictures of the showrooms at Daneway
House.

As near as possible, by borrowing back the furniture from art galleries and
private homes, they re-created those showroom displays of 1904. We were
invited, too.

All these buildings have links ...

This is <u>Beechanger</u>, in a lovely position to the east of the Church. It was Sidney Barnsley's choice. He also designed the Gyde Almshouses at Painswick.

<u>Daneway House</u> became their showroom.

... with the "School of Sapperton Craftsmen".

rnest Barnsley decided he would like to build on to an
xisting cottage for the home of his choice. <u>Upper Dorvel</u>
<u>ouse</u> was the result. The original building at the centre
nay have been the house in a similar position on
he old etching of Sapperton House.

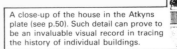

A close-up of the house in the Atkyns
plate (see p.50). Such detail can prove to
be an invaluable visual record in tracing
the history of individual buildings.

Ernest Gimson built the <u>Leasowes</u> for himself. The Craftsmen endeared themselves to the local people by being enthusiastic participants in all village activities including amateur dramatics.

This 17th-century house (upper picture), the Bell Inn
(pre 1781) and Manor Farm (right) are a few more examples of our houses of interest.

We hope you have enjoyed being with us as we explored our past. We believe many communities have a similar rich and varied heritage.

We have it because people in the past cared enough ... to look after their buildings, land and records so that these things are preserved for us to see today.

They cared. They conserved.

We must be conservation - conscious, too. We have already said the heart of the village is protected. £25,000 has been spent restoring the Church. The Village Hall (of "Craftsman" design) is being refurbished and restored.

But what about us?

What about the Village School?

When the sands in the hourglass run low, will people remember that we, too, with our traditions, have tried to be a worthy part of the heritage of Sapperton?

We hope they will conserve us, too......

These pictures show us receiving the Group Section Prize (Bledisloe Cup 1981) for a scrapbook entitled "Our Village Story."

Our story is so fascinating that we long to share it with the many visitors and friends who come to Sapperton each year.

To do it justice we believe it should be well presented, in full colour; yet such an undertaking would be financially beyond the reach of a small village school like ours, numbering only 26 pupils. So we sought, as did artists in days gone by, a patron who would sponsor this work, so that more may realise what a debt is owed to those in the past, who have cared, conserved and loved: Sapperton - Our Village Heritage.

An Appreciation :

is with deep gratitude and excitement that I write this postscript to our book.

the summer of 1984 we submitted it for a competition organised by the Country Landowners sociation. They thought it so worthy of publication they offered to be part sponsors of the cost. we sought for others to share this not inconsiderable sum, the Ernest Cook Charitable Trust o became one of our principal sponsors. This gave us the incentive to continue our search others and we gratefully present these sponsors with our thanks for enabling us to sent this quality volume :

The Country Landowners Charitable Trust,

Country Landowners Glos. Branch,

The Ernest Cook Trust,

The Diocese of Gloucester,

Sapperton Parish Council,

English Heritage,

. & V. James,

Frederick Wills Charitable Trust,

National Association for the Support of Small Schools,

Langtree Charitable Trust,

The Earl Bathurst,

The Charles Wolfson Charitable Trust,

Gloucestershire Education Committee,

Rural Initiative Fund,

Rev. W. Woodhouse,

Bruce Ball Charitable Trust,

Ken Gardner,

J. H. Parker,

Oscar Guggenheim.

Sapperton School watch their manuscript on its way to becoming a book.

would also like to thank Alan Sutton and Peter Clifford, Publishing Director, for recognising potential in r work in the early days and Michael Wood for his wonderful involvement. Of course, the book could not have been npiled without the full co-operation of all the villagers in Sapperton. We hope they will be as thrilled with this ished work as we are, P.M. Pinnell, Headteacher, Sapperton C. of E. School, near Cirencester, Gloucestershire.

We are grateful to all who have helped us make this book. Most sources are acknowledged in the text but we would like to extend special thanks to the following advisors who actually "steered" us towards many of these sources :-

James Meadows, Warden of the South Gloucestershire
                                                Teachers' Centre, Stroud.
Bryan Jerrard, Chairman, County Local History Committee,
Jean Welsford, Warden, Cirencester Teachers' Centre,
Cynthia Cooksey, Regional Education Officer of
                                                "English Heritage,
Alan Morley, Divisional Librarian, Stroud.